from Beloit
to Clark Gable
in Three
Generations

Dearest Pat,

My dear friend, I hope
you enjoy the read. You
inspire me !

Love —

Dianna

First edition   August 2024

Copyright © 2024   Dianna Jackson

                     travelswiththerayman.com

Published by Penciled In

5319 Barrenda Ave

Atascadero, CA 93422

penciledin.com

ISBN-13:   978-1-939502-63-6

Book and Cover Design by Benjamin Daniel Lawless.   ⌃

Text is set in Arno Pro, Canela Text and Californian FB.

from Beloit to Clark Gable in Three Generations

A FAMILY MEMOIR

Dianna Jackson

Contents

Introduction

Well, it took a lifetime, but I finally figured out my purpose in life and why, as a not-yet-born baby, I had single-handedly jiggled my way around to an upright position in the uterus of my mother so that my feet came out first. And for years, this has been a pattern oft repeated as I found my way in the world. Going the wrong way first.

Having said that, this story may have been written earlier if I hadn't engaged in doing absolutely everything humanly possible to make mistake after mistake, guaranteeing a sort-of "Why do it the easy way, when I can take the harder way instead" lifestyle.

The road is littered with people like me. You, dear reader, might be one of them, so you know what I mean. If not, self-congratulation is in order. And I don't mind telling you that you are smart as the dickens (whatever that means).

The subject at hand is the story I am writing, which attempts to explain how in the world it came to be that I was born feet-down in a town with a mud hole.

The story starts in Beloit, Wisconsin, in the mid-1800s. That is where my great-great-grandfather and great-great-grandmother lived and had their children, five in all... a minor miracle in itself because my great-great-grandmother, Sarah Jenks Dresser, was a sickly woman. William Henry Dresser was a man gripped in the dream of moving west and spent stretches of time in Madison, Wisconsin, the territory's capital, pulling teeth and taking lantern pictures to make enough money to follow his nose to California during the Gold Rush. He had a bout of gold fever and would not be deterred. Sarah, who spent much of her young life bearing his children, declined the opportunity to cross the plains because of her fear of the unknown.

In this day and age, it is hard to even imagine such a trip, but let's take a stab at it anyway. While grapevines were being planted by the friars at the missions of California, William and Sarah were listening to the grapevines they knew, and those consisted of human beings telling tales—some true, some rumors, some outlandish, some within the cloak of credulity. They got their information from friends, family, and newspapers. Radio had not been invented, Walter Cronkite was not on the still-to-be-invented technology of television, and neither had GPS become a technology used by millions. Things were so uncomplicated, I don't think it surprising that people provided their own entertainment, which apparently included sex and playing the piano.

But the die had been cast. William was looking for a better life for himself and his family. He was an educated White man, so things worked out for him much better than for the Native American man. Or the poor Black man ripped from the African continent for a life of misery in what was labeled "indentured servitude," preferring that euphemism over the ugly term "slavery." William had the freedom to roam. He had an education and could read and write. And he did both with great gusto. It happened that he wrote dear Sarah letters while away from hearth and home. First there were letters that were posted from Madison, Wisconsin territory in 1847 as he had traveled there to make money for his excursion west. He rented a room in the Madison Hotel, not far from the building that the good people of the territory of Wisconsin met in to hash out the articles of the Constitution for the soon-to-become state of Wisconsin. In that hotel, while the men (and they were all men) made up the rules of state government, William Henry was busy pulling teeth and taking pictures.

DENTISTRY.

SAVE YOUR TEETH !

WILLIAM DRESSER,

SURGEON DENTIST, can be found at the Madison Hotel, fully prepared to operate on teeth in any or all the various modes of cleaning, filling and inserting teeth by pivot and plate work. Particular attention paid to diseased gums. Do not let Procrastination rob you of your teeth and deform that human face divine. Advice free. Prices to suit the times.
Madison, Dec. 1, 1847.

He was not alone. There was a bevy of men, and some women, preparing to take off for Cala, as they nicknamed the place, California. Companies were formed, plans were forged, and people were very excited at the prospect of prospecting.

Thanks to the letters that William and Sarah exchanged as he trudged across the plains, I found out why I was born in Atascadero, California. And I discovered what a hell of a journey it was. But I was arm-chairing it in the comfort of my home. As a native Californian, I had not been to Beloit. Nor had I been to the places William Henry came across and then wrote about on his journey. Therefore, I had no appreciation of the ground he traveled. On the other hand, he was not the first. Native Americans had trampled down trails to be followed year after year as they traveled the great land they inhabited, so their expertise and knowledge helped those like my family to find the way. Good news for the White man, bad news for the Native. And, of course, the Mormons blazed the trails as they fled religious persecution in search of their promised land. People like my great-great-grandfather left England in the early 1800s, some much earlier, to escape various man-made persecutions. The weather wasn't that great in the British Isles, either. And there was always a religious leader who was more than happy to get his (yes, always always a man) flock to a state of disenchantment so that his followers would feel a need to move.

So, what to do? After writing the first draft of this book, I met a woman much brighter than me, who probably wasn't born feet first in a town with a "mud hole" and may have made good choices in her life. After I described the book I was writing, she popped up with the idea that since I had been blogging for years with a readership of about five loyal friends, I should blend the book with my blogging and take a trip back to Beloit where William Henry Dresser both started his family and his trip west, and tell the story that way.

And so that is what I did. Hitting the trail took on its intended meaning and has shaped my life in a new and exciting way. Because I must confess, I almost flunked American history as a student at San Jose State in the 1960s. History was my least favorite class. Memorizing names and dates seemed senseless to me.

Now look at me. My great-great-grandparents led me in countless ways to this moment. And I am thrilled at the prospect of discovering the path—with the aid of GPS, hotels, hot water, and hiking boots.

For purposes of this book, William Henry Dresser and Sarah Dresser comprise the first generation of my American roots.

This is the map of the Mormon Trail
produced by the National Park Service (NPS)

The map was very useful in following in the
footsteps of William Henry Dresser. It may be
a page to dog-ear for the reader to reference.
The trail did not end there for most emigrants.
It was used for most Mormon settlers,
however. More maps will follow.

Prologue

In the early '60s, while hippies were celebrating the Summer of Love, my grandmother told me that my ancestors had written letters and those letters were located in the Bancroft Library at UC Berkeley, the campus where all hell broke loose when student sit-ins thrust the university into the national spotlight. Academically, the university had already secured the spotlight for academic prowess. Sit-ins were the focus of the new spotlight.

Discovery of this information piqued my interest. However, I was too busy making poor choices, so all I did was let the knowledge flounder about in my head for years before I actually got the gumption to go find the letters.

Libraries are quiet. And none more so in my experience than Bancroft Library on the University of California's Berkeley's campus. Dripping in serious scholarship, this place was more like a cathedral for brains. It was here that I traveled in the 1980s to look at letters.

The letters were bequeathed to the school in 1963 by Dorothy Cartwright Piez and Beatrice Cartwright Crist, two great granddaughters of William Henry. As I read some of the letters, It became quite apparent that I must own copies of this material.

With a habit of chomping on #2 lead pencils painted yellow while in the throes of contemplation, I had run out of fresh places to chomp. This drove me to the conclusion that all this was just too much to read in one sitting, and too much to absorb at first glance. Lucky for me, the university was in the business of offering Xerox copies of all the material. What was included was a copy of each original letter with postmarked envelopes, and a copy of a transcribed version, typed. The originals were extremely delicate and had lots of spelling and grammatical errors. This made reading the originals very difficult. Some letters were written by candlelight and the candle had burned so low, according to one of my great-great-grandfather's letters, he had to close for the night because the paper was on fire. In total, there were twenty nine letters to Sarah, and Sarah authored nine letters to him. Page 16 is a copy of an original letter. There may have been more but if there were, they were not given to the university.

An example is shown below:

Fort Laramie May 29/50

Dear Sarah

It is with pleasure that I have an oportunity to write to you although it is imposable to say when you will receive this as it will not leave this place until the return mail from the Bluffs to Salt Lake passes here, which left that place (the Bluffs) ten dayes before we did. I feel thankfull to the Allwise Providence that my health is as good as I could wish and well it might for a healthier country than this place to the Missourie the Sun neaver shone on. no accident as happened to us man or beast except one man's horse got to wheat (feed) in the night and eat so much that he kit the bucket. The season thus far is very backward, the grass did not furnish a good bite untill we came on the North branch of the Platt on the 23rd then we enjoyed the lucsury of some Glorious Showers, and two tremendous blows the rest of the time greatly to my surprise the rest of the time the weather has been mild and remarkably pleasant it is true this has been the halcyon dayes, nature's own repose The vally of the Platt is unique, buitfull, and healthy beyond description with the exception of some 3 or 4 places where the Bluffs come down to the river, each 6 or 8 miles over sandy hills, the road is a perfect inclined plane assending as we pass up the river the banks being but a few feet above the surface of the river, the bottoms are generaly about ten miles wide a good soil easely cultivated not so rich as the best land in Winnebago Co the bluffs and all the land back of the botoms as far as we have eny knowledge is a sucksession of sand hills with sufficien grass for sheep pasture if they could have roon enough, but good for nothing if once ploughed a considerable cotton wood timber on the banks and numerous isleands. The country on the North branch is quite different, the bluffs are abbrupt composed of an earth which I cant describe a mixture of clay and sand softer than chalk some of it nearly as white in emence solled boddeyes, and sufficiently tenacious to make the cheapest building material I ever saw, some specimens might nead a coat of plaster to prevent the action of the weather but I think not, up to the forks 300 miles not a stone to throw at a bird nor a rock of aney kind from the forks 200 miles not a stick to beat a dog with except a very few scanty willows depended on Buffaloe chips and found them good enough, in the vicinity of the forks found thousands of Buffaloes we had the finest fun in the world hunting them I shot a fine young cow, Oh how I did wish Abby & Charley to see the fun fun it was sure enough notwithstanding they would sometimes take their

So, what did I do with these copies?
Nothing. For years I did nothing. I didn't even
read them. Another bad choice on my part.
They were filed in a binder and placed on a
shelf as I busied myself doing stupid things at
my job with the phone company. Inane, stupid
things that someone else should have done.
Correction, stupid things that no one should
have done.

Eventually, my interest was piqued. Hey,
but not so fast. It piqued slowly, very slowly,
like a sloth moving up a tree. Or down a tree.
Before I turned my flashlight on the history
contained in the binder of letters, I had to first
be told I had no idea what I was talking about.
This happened when my husband, Rayman
(aka Ray), and I discussed the Israeli-
Palestinian conflict in the late '90s. I sided
with the Israelis. He, the Palestinians. But he
was a history buff. As a kid he read
encyclopedias for fun. And he absorbed
information like a sponge with a brain. I had a
profound admiration for his cerebral powers

and whenever I didn't know a historical tidbit, he was always there to save the day (before Google and after). He just knew history.

Exasperated with me, he finally said, "I don't think you know what you are talking about regarding the history of the Middle East. Perhaps you should do some reading." I could not disagree. So, I took up some nonfiction reading. *From Beirut to Jerusalem* was my first serious foray into history. Thank you, Thomas Friedman. And the list of history books grew. *The Rise and Fall of the Third Reich* was gobbled up one summer as I lay on the couch of our RV out in the woods. And on it went. Until one day, I got the notion to read the history that was stored in a binder on a shelf of my own house. A binder of letters that were the real deal.

Madison Hotel Madison Octr 26, 1847

My Dear Sarah

"Tis painfuly pleasing" to thus communicate while fate or
fortune divides us and forbids more intimate and pleasent communion.
I arrived here as expected on thursday about 4 PM having had a very
agreable journey, my helth is good excepting that the could I had
when I left home increased considerably both in my head & on my
longs but it is subsiding quite fast it has mostly left my head & I
have been storming it on my longs with Hoarhound candy but it is
something like the Mexicanoes hates to give up. likeing the fun, but
I think my cough is getting better sloly It was imposible to get
the promis of a room to work in until after the close of the present
short session of the legislature for les than ten Dollars per week
and that at but one place and thank God their was no more such; but
by the politenes and real kindnes of a br odd Felleow a member of
the Legeslatioun I got posesion of a good room on Monday morning
(yesterday) and on that day fitted it up in full and today
commenced in full blast, had 4 customers but they put it of quite
late and I accommodated 2, one was a distinquished member who took
it into the bar room and shewed its sitisons & strangers (the room
being full) and it was pronounced perfect I am toled he is at
another tavern exibiting it and it is receiving great aplause, I am
doeing some work for a very populor Minister who promises much for
me by way of influence—I cant have less then a dozen positive
engagements and this is my first day if you should be able to send
with all posible speed for more stock I fear they would not reach
me soon enough I have maney warm friends scatered through the town
odd Fellows the Welches, both are and are doing their best for me as
in fact they did last spring—Court is now in Session which will
last 2 or 3 weeks which is bringing vast numbers here—very soon
after that is through the convention will set then in the middle of
winter the regular Sessions of the Legislator these all help the
sitison to cash and brings in a vast number of casuall people You
see my predicament Lay these things before Br Brown and tell him
he can and must be promt he must not waver a moment and tel James
that I will have him and Dan turned out of the lodge if they don't
rase $ on that of Traiton's brothy. perhaps you can borow 1, 2, or 3
dollars of Friend Hance if it is necessary—make a raise out of the
tallow enny how; I can send the money in a very few days to replace
enny thing you may want—without something turns out very bad I must
do very fair buisness but the prospects are very flatering indeed
only think of the present prospects without a single hand bill up ask
James to urge Wilkeson to finish any sign I want it bad, as to that
affair of Uncle Joels dont do anything att all until you write to me
first letters very soon pass eastern mails leave here everyday and
sometimes twice this is my desire—It is now about 10 oclk and I

So, I read them. And they percolated. And they percolated some more. And finally it occurred to me that there were stories to tell. I was related to the authors. If I didn't tell the story, others might. Silly me. A book, *The Dresser Letters*,[1] a group on Facebook entitled *Dresser Family Descendants of William Dresser 1813 - 1894*, and a newspaper article existed unbeknownst to me until I had written part of this book.

But here's the thing. All roads are connected. If you get lost, you can get found. And that is why before I started writing about history, I was busy making history with the Rayman in the form of blogs about our travel misadventures.

Travelswiththerayman.com became a "thing." It was great fun, and so that got me writing for, yes, myself, but also for anyone who had ever been caught being a human being while traveling. Traveling takes a person

---

[1] Decottignies , Becky. *The Dresser Letters*, Lulu Press, July 20, 2013

out of their comfort zone, and Rayman gave me plenty of material to work with. He refused to go to Mexico until we went to Mexico and he loved it. He didn't want to drive across the country until we did. And we have the blogs to prove it. Having grown up in Virginia, which he did not leave until the war in Vietnam commenced and he had enlisted in the Air Force to avoid being cannon fodder in the Army, he didn't stray far from home. Adventure was not his middle name. Ironic for someone who ended up flying to Vietnam to wire runway lights, yes? But here's the thing. Uncle Sam was in control. It was structure, discipline, and free room and board. Left to his own devices, he may never have left the South had it not been for the war.

My acquired maternal family history (back as far I really care to go) began in Europe. My great-great-grandfather was the son of a linen maker in London. He floated over with his family to Montreal when he was a lad. They moved to northern New York and the new land, called America, and from there found their way to Beloit. But that wasn't enough. He wanted more.

Let the journey begin.

The First Generation

"Life should not be a journey to the grave with the intention of arriving safely in a pretty and well-preserved body, but rather to skid in broadside in a cloud of smoke, thoroughly used up, totally worn out, and loudly proclaiming, "wow! What a ride!"

— HUNTER S. THOMPSON

CHAPTER ONE:
WILLIAM AND SARAH DRESSER

Every man has his own destiny: the only imperative is to follow it, to accept it, no matter where it leads him.

— HENRY MILLER

William Henry Dresser, my great-great-grandfather (GGGF) on my mom's side, was born in East Smithfield, London, on August 20, 1813. Christopher and Mary Dresser were his parents. After his family lost two homes to fire, and his mother and a brother died of consumption, his father moved out of London in search of a better life... to Malton in County York. Apparently things didn't work out so well for these Dressers in England; they arrived in Montreal, Canada, on June 30, 1824. The ship manifest recorded that Christopher was with two boys, two girls, and a wife. William Henry, my great-great-grandfather, was just eleven years old.

From there William Henry moved with his dad, mom, and siblings to New York and then on to Boone County, Illinois. However, William Henry did not move with the family directly to Illinois. He stopped off at Allegheny College in Pennsylvania to study before completing the move. Smart fellow, he was. I was able to confirm his attendance at Allegheny College. He did not graduate but he did attend according to Linda Lees of the Alumni Engagement at Allegheny College.

Under what circumstances he met and married my great-great-grandmother (GGGmother), Sarah Jenks, remains unknown. However, with the help of myriad historical societies, I was able to find the property records for the Jenks family at 5267 High Street, in Roscoe, Illinois.

For purposes of this book, William Henry Dresser and Sarah Dresser comprise the first generation of my American roots.

I have copies of envelopes postmarked to Sarah and sent to Beloit in 1848. Then the address changes from Beloit, to Roscoe, Illinois. With some literary license, I have deduced that when William Henry went charging off into the sunset, Sarah moved close to her family, the Jenks. And anyway, titling the book *From Roscoe to Clark Gable* doesn't have the same ring to it as *From Beloit to Clark Gable*.

Finally, Beloit and Roscoe are only seven miles apart. And they were only seven miles apart then too. So, the family lived close by and the man-made state, county, and city lines hardly made a difference.

Henry Miller's quote at the beginning of

this chapter references men. "Men" in this quote also implies "women" (from my view). That is how I applied it here.

Before delving deeper, let me explain that I am not a trained historian. Therefore this book is not, by definition, scholarly. However, it is accurate as far as I know and it has humor because humor makes my day and I hope it makes yours too.

Every effort was made to determine and verify the facts of history. Many books were read in order to complete this work. There are some footnotes. Ellipses. Asterisks (*) included to illustrate points made and provide references as necessary. My main objective was to entertain and inform. Hope I was successful!

CHAPTER TWO:
SOME BACKGROUND ON THE GOLD RUSH

"During the gold rush it's a good time to be in the pick and shovel business."

— MARK TWAIN

The California Gold Rush launched an enormous migration of people who were searching for a better life. According to John D. Unruh, Jr., author of *The Plains Across: The Overland Emigrant and The Trans-Mississippi West, 1840-60*, "in 1849, 25,000 people arrived in California from the East. In 1850, 44,000 people made the journey. And by the time that 1860 rolled around, 200,335 people had arrived in California."[2] Perhaps the numbers don't seem so high today. However, what it

---

[2] Unruh, Jr., John D, *The Plains Across: The Overland Emigrant and The Trans-Mississippi West, 1840-60*, (Champaign, University Illinois Press, 1979), 120.

took to make that journey seems truly remarkable to this kid. In the same book is the following comment to help paint the picture more clearly, "Mr. James D. Persinger reported that their company passed 200 wagons early one 1850 morning, were passed by another 100 another noon, and passed at least 500 more another day."[3] The number of people in each wagon varied.

Dr. Reuben Knox, writing from near Fort Kearny, Nebraska territory, reported that 1,000 wagons passed on the last day of May 1850.[4]

For these men, women, and children, the trip required careful planning and, of course, money. William Henry needed the resources to embark on such an adventure and at the same time provide for Sarah and the children. How did he do this?

In 1847 he traveled to Madison, Wisconsin, territory to set up shop in order to earn money

[3] Unruh, Jr., John, 120.
[4] Unruh, Jr., John, 120.

taking pictures and pulling teeth. Wisconsin was in the throes of transitioning from a territory into a state. On page 36 is a newspaper ad William Henry placed in the newspaper of the time. He was a photographer by hobby and turned this hobby into a money-making venture. According to the Smithsonian and I quote; "When photography emerged in the mid-1800s, it was a natural fit for the "Magic Lantern" technology. Basically, a photographic lantern slide is a positive print of a photograph on a glass slide. Often times the photographic negatives were painstakingly hand-colored to make them even more visually enticing. Many photographic lantern slides were also "matted" by a piece of opaque paper laid on the slide, which both masked out edges or parts of the image not wanted in the frame, and created the desirable aesthetic appearance of a mounted photograph. Finally, a second slide of glass was laid atop the glass slide with the positive print and these two pieces of glass were bound firmly together by pasting a strip of paper around the edges. The sandwiched glass plates held the matte or mask in place and also protected the positive photographic print from dust, scratches, and the like. The final slide was then ready to be viewed in a lantern slide projector. Photographic lantern slides took off in the late 19th century as a popular form of entertainment, and in addition to educators, missionaries and salespeople soon began to use Magic Lantern slides to visually entice the audience while educating, spreading their messages, and peddling their wares. In this sense, lantern slides were a kind of precursor to the Power Point presentations we're all so familiar with now."

In the same manner as the advertisement for his photography, he also paid for an ad to draw attention to his pastime as a dentist. I was unable to find any documentation that he had a degree in dentistry. The advertisement, however, verifies that he did offer his services.

COLORED OR PLAIN
Photographic Miniatures,
TAKEN BY WM. DRESSER.

AT the *MADISON HOTEL*, in the latest and most approved style, having one of the most splendid instruments ever brought to the West. Please call and examine specimens.

Instructions given in the art, and apparatus furnished on reasonable terms.

I love the line, "Prices to suit the times." His skills as a dentist may have only been exceeded by his marketing prowess and his considerable chutzpah.

Writing to Sarah often from Madison, he set the tone for the first half of his life as a man of letters. It appears that he fell into the habit of writing while traveling. He wrote to both request and provide help. He asked for chemicals for developing photos and he sent money for the children. And he was a religious teetotaler. The letter on the next page illustrates these points.

Madison Hotel Madison Octr 26, 1847

My Dear Sarah

"Tis painfuly pleasing" to thus communicate while fate or
fortune divides us and forbids more intimate and pleasent communion.
I arrived here as expected on thursday about 4 PM having had a very
agreable journey, my helth is good excepting that the could I had
when I left home increased considerably both in my head & on my
longs but it is subsiding quite fast it has mostly left my head & I
have been storming it on my longs with Hoarhound candy but it is
something like the Mexicanoes hates to give up. likeing the fun, but
I think my cough is getting better sloly It was imposible to get
the promis of a room to work in until after the close of the present
short session of the legislature for les than ten Dollars per week
and that at but one place and thank God their was no more such; but
by the politenes and real kindnes of a br odd Felleow a member of
the Legeslatioun I got posesion of a good room on Monday morning
(yesterday) and on that day fitted it up in full and today
commenced in full blast, had 4 customers but they put it of quite
late and I accommodated 2, one was a distinquished member who took
it into the bar room and shewed its sitisons & strangers (the room
being full) and it was pronounced perfect I am toled he is at
another tavern exibiting it and it is receiving great aplause, I am
doeing some work for a very populor Minister who promises much for
me by way of influence—I cant have less then a dozen positive
engagements and this is my first day if you should be able to send
with all posible speed for more stock I fear they would not reach
me soon enough I have maney warm friends scatered through the town
odd Fellows the Welches, both are and are doing their best for me as
in fact they did last spring—Court is now in Session which will
last 2 or 3 weeks which is bringing vast numbers here—very soon
after that is through the convention will set then in the middle of
winter the regular Sessions of the Legislator these all help the
sitison to cash and brings in a vast number of casuall people You
see my predicament Lay these things before Br Brown and tell him
he can and must be promt he must not waver a moment and tel James
that I will have him and Dan turned out of the lodge if they don't
rase $ on that of Traiton's broth. perhaps you can borow 1, 2, or 3
dollars of Friend Hance if it is necessary—make a raise out of the
tallow enny how; I can send the money in a very few days to replace
enny thing you may want—without something turns out very bad I must
do very fair buisness but the prospects are very flatering indeed
only think of the present prospects without a single hand bill up ask
James to urge Wilkeson to finish any sign I want it bad, as to that
affair of Uncle Joels dont do anything att all until you write to me
first letters very soon pass eastern mails leave here everyday and
sometimes twice this is my desire—It is now about 10 oclk and I

Did he know that he was going West in 1847? This is a question unanswered. The Madison letters do not mention his thinking on the subject. When he returns home, the letters stop and so does our knowledge of his intent.

He was thirty-four years old in 1847. It may be inferred that he had experience at farming since that was the assumed livelihood for most people in Beloit. He owned pigs and cows and had an understanding of good land. We know from his young life that he had experience in traveling. That he made the decision to join the Gold Rush is a fact. I think he wanted more in life for his family and saw that striking it rich was a fantastic opportunity that was worth both the time and the risk.

As most emigrants were wont to do, he joined a group or the group joined him in forming a "company" to make the journey. His group was identified as Fargo, Carter and Otis.

Because "Dresser"[5] was listed as a traveler in this group, I'm of the opinion that he joined their group. In this manner, costs of the trip were shared and in reading other accounts, this form of organization was much used by most emigrants. In the account of a Mr. Bruff[6] (written starting in 1849), Mr. Bruff travels with a very large group of mostly twenty-somethings, nearly six dozen of them. Together they assembled $11,000 which in today's dollars would be $446,617. Because Mr. Bruff formed his company in Washington, D.C., for fact-finding and research, he was in charge and actually did a masterful job handling all circumstances thrown his way.

[5] *The book of Beloit*, [1836-1936]. (1936). [Beloit, Wis.]: Daily News Publishing Co.

[6] *Gold Rush: The Journals, Drawings, and Other Papers of J. Goldsborough Bruff, Captain, Washington City and California Mining Association, April 2, 1849–July 20, 1851.* Edited by Georgia Willis Read and Ruth Gaines. With a Foreword by F. W. Hodge. Volume I, Washington City to Bruff's Camp. Volume II, Bruff–s Camp To Washington City. (New York: Columbia University Press. 1944.

With the money William Henry raised, the plan was to set off with his partners. There are no letters by William Henry that spelled out the plan. The first we know of his plan looking back, is the letter he penned from Council Bluffs, then known as Kanesville, dated May 1, 1850. Kanesville is known today as Council Bluffs, Iowa.

Kaynesville, May 1st/50

My Dear Sarah

   I fear you will think my delay rather long before you receive
this, I have had nothing of importance to write. When we arrived
at Monro I Bot half of N Otis team and all that appertained
theireto, one fourth of all the provisions tent, stove, cooking
utensils etc that Fargo, Carter & Otis had I paid him (Otis) One
hundred and five Dollars cash, twelve Dollars in dried meat, and
gave him my note for forty seven Dollars more than for the cash
expenses and the price of another horse I shall be still indebted
to him, whatever the establishment will fitch will help pay back
this outfit, we now expect that it will be occonemey prity soon
after crosing the Rocky Mountains to throw away our waggon and
pack through there being a nearer rout discovered by the Mormans
last fall which can be packed a little more than half the time
that waggons can pas the other road if I had known before I had
started what I now know I should come here by water bot 2
horses and packed all the way I might of stayed at home 3 weeks
longer; in fact comeing as we did we would have done better to
have stayed at home ten days longer, people were not only crazy
mad but were fools at that for they would not proffit by
experience, we very soon found that we were to early and we fooled
away most of the seccond week, and now we are altogether to early,
we got here some 5 hours over 3 week from the time we started we
shall hardly leave here before the first of next week, the wither
is very cold water fros in the pail last night more than 1/2 inch
thick, there is scarce any grass at all in the Sloughs about enough
on the dry prairie to pasture goats I don't know that I ever saw the
grass [   ] forward on the Rolling than the wet prairie, nearly
all through Iowa the land is similiar to De'Kalb Co Ill the
greatest [expectation] is that it is more Rolling, the Prairies are
very rich and emencly large the distance from Beloit here is 470
for near the last 300 miles there was a very sparce settlement
quite lattey settled (about 3 years) without grain or hay we had
to lay in our grain and hall it the whol of that distance without
hay for our horses, of course our horses lost considerable flesh,
we only past 4 dead horses we pased the grave of one man from
Racine and heard of the death of one from Belvidere the former
caught cold which terminated in inflamation on the Longues the
other sleeping in his waggon a cold rain fell on his head which
induced inflamation in the head—those who started so early were
much more exposed than we have been twice there has been rain
enough to lay the dust and that is all, if we could only have a
good rain and terminate warm we should have grass very soon—If we
don't have rain within 2 or 3 weeks we shalnot have the pleasure of

a good drenching until we catch it from the winter rains in the
diggins for we are informed that scarce ever rains on the plains
or in fact on the whole rout after leaving here a week or 2 or 3.
I have had conversations with several who have past and repast
the whole distance and I cant find anything to dread, any great
hardships to encounter, I have enquired much for the most
dificult things that we have to encounter and am not able to find
what they are, we meet with meny women and children with happy
and bouyant harts bound for Cal͟a and Origon, with refference to
Cal͟a our health, ultimate success, and everything pertaing to our
great enterpris I wish you would obtain Hon T. Butler King's
Report on Calafornia to J. M. Clayton Secy of State and read it
and then do as I did studyit all over the second time, excepting
that part (the introduction) pertaining to the state Government,
you will find it in the N. Y. Tribune of Apr. 6 or many other
subsequent papers, we have had no sickness among us and the
emigration as·far as I can learn is very healthy, some 3 or 4 have
had the small pox but it has been so light that some dispute its
being small pox but it is small pox no doubt some few dayes we
had to cross a good many sloughs otherwayes the roads were as good
as roads could well be many not accoustome to them some mired the
horses and broke there waggons but Otis & I have not broke the
first thing neither have our horses been sick. We are told that
we shall be obliged to keep a strict watch every night to keep the
Indians from stealing horses beyond that we have nothing to fear I
wish you [could] send a doller to Br Adams the Methodist preacher
I mean the.painter for my dues to the S. of Tempeence if you
don't hear anything to the contrary 3 months hence send one
doller more. Mills gave you three Dollars I presume that I gave
him for you, you have probably got the auger and draw knife from
Clements the Gouldsmith and the chisels from Lancaster, Cemera
did not pay that fifteen dollars as he agreed the buisness is all
at Br Easterly cousin friend Mills to see to that for you,
Healy told me that he would pay George out of the store or any
other way enytime some ten Dollars; I would say that I forgot to
pay my dues to the Son͟s,—And when I wrote to James I forgot to tell
him about Saxby, Old Downer is witness to the bargain and B
Hackett & Drake heard him agree to meet me at there rooms to do the
work at three o'clk the friday previous to my departure which he
neglected to do so I filled my part of the Contract Hackett sayed
that Sacksby could not enforce payment I dont know when I shall
write to James again please transcribe what I have writen about
this affair & what ever would be interesting in this letter to him—
I left that French buisnes with he had a clame of $2.00 When he
collects it from French he will be entitled to 3 Dollers more
$5.00. I gave the butcher a chance in for about $4.00 & Dexter $3
more makeing in all $12 now if this is ever got and you could get
the ballance (which is rather doubtfull) there would be some $15
for you, trying will cast nothing stick to it and keep trying, if

a judgement is obtained rather than let others get hold of it lit
him satisfy the above claimes then perhaps by throwing of a quarter
he would be induced to pay directly to you now these fellows will
be on the allert and will surely catch French and get a judgement,
the trick will be to get the rest yourself As to the enterprise in
which we are engaged there is everything to encourage and nothing
to discourage in the common course of human events, after much
inquiry I find that the only great dificulty that I had to
encounter was surmounted when friend George with that true
generosaty found only in a true and humble heart (may God grant
that I may be enabled to reciprocate the favour) lent me that money—
I shall not write until just before we leave — There can hardly be
said to be any town at the Bluffs this is a Mean Mormon Hole 8
miles from one fery some 6 stores & a host of Helleryes filled
with beastly drunkenness May 9th We are now on the Banks of the
river of Mud (Missourie) we have left the Beloit Co (i e Fargo,
Carter, Otis & myself for the purpose of goin with Mr Hicks of
Elkhorn Walworth Co Wis who has just returned got his wife and
returning you can gudge of the dreadfull hardships I have seen
several men returning to Cal with their wives my only wish is that
you and the children were with me,we cross today expecting to leave in
a day or two Cap Hicks sayes he will put us through in 70 dayes.
Emediatly on the receipt of this write to San Francisco We have
Bot a horse pritty good for $40. We found one spot of good grass
last 4 dayes horses done well I shall write from Salt Lake, and now
I want to say something to my Boyes tel Albert & Charley not to
forget Pa and Love one another I am writing in the waggon with
hundreds around me and my eyes forbid me writing mutch tel Lanney to
give Tilley a good kiss for Pa, Give my respects to All and believe me

Your affectionate husband
Wm Dresser

P S

Get some one to get our letters from the Methodist Church and
attach to Roscoe I intended to get my letter but forgot it pray
for me and yourself and children and I will do the same every day
that God may grant that we may yet enjoy each others company untill
we are taken hence

W D

Addressed to: Postmark: Nebraska Iowa May 13

    Mrs Sarah Dresser   Postage: 10¢
    Roscoe Winnebago Ill

As he pushed headlong toward the west, he left Sarah and his children in Beloit. The family was as follows:

- Sarah Jenks Dresser and William Henry, wed July 29, 1838.
- Albert Richard Dresser, born Sept. 13, 1839
- Charles Harris Dresser, born April 22, 1842
- Emma Matilda Dresser, born 1845
- **William Orlando Dresser, born May 11, 1847**
- Julia Mariah Dresser, born Dec. 10, 1850

He left Sarah with all four children when he went to Madison, Wisconsin, in 1847. And he left Sarah with them again, when he headed west. In reading her letters, I just want to cry. Everything falls to her. Yes, her mother was nearby, as were other family members. However, the trip west was a big ask, so I guess that was that. I most certainly owe her a debt of gratitude.

Recently the Wisconsin Historical Society shared an article with me that appeared in the Milwaukee Journal, August 5, 1934… *"Graphic story of the Rush to California told in the letters of a Wisconsin pioneer"* which adds the following information:

"Across the scattered fringe of an excited little Wisconsin village named Beloit, there moved a covered wagon: Others led, still others followed. Its sturdy timbers groaned beneath a heavy load. Its ponderous wheels yielded grotesque mud pies to a host of shouting, scrambling farmer boys running beside it.

"This was the year 1850 and an upright bearded giant leaned far out of the driver's seat and waved a hand to rearward. Somewhere in Beloit, a woman, sobbing children clinging to her gingham apron, waved back.

"Neither could see the other. It might be that eyes would never again meet eyes. They loved each other, this man and this woman. So much did she love him even at that wrenching press of his iron lips upon the quivering softness of her own, she had not divulged the secret: There was to be yet another baby. If he knew, he would stay."[7]

I am uncertain who wrote this article. Was it my great-great-grandfather? This information illustrates what the family sacrificed and how selfless Sarah was at that moment.

William Orlando Dresser, listed above in bold print on page 44 was my great-grandfather and part of the second generation of the Dresser family. You will learn more about him in section two.

So, off went William Henry. He wrote to Sarah from Fort Laramie, Wyoming on May 29,1850. He was in the business of passing and being passed by a multitude of wagons, all pulled by oxen, horses, mules. Most of the travelers preferred oxen because they were strong and could pull the heavy wagons loaded

---

[7] Wisconsin Historical Society. Wisconsin Local History & Biography Articles; "Milwaukee Journal"; "Milwaukee", "Wisconsin"; "August 5, 1934"; viewed online at https://www.wisconsinhistory.org on May 21, 2024]

down with household items: food to eat, food for the animals to eat, spare parts for the wagons, guns for protection, and family possessions that they could not part with on the journey. Items to trade with the Native Americans were also carried in many wagons.

This is a picture sketched by William Henry Jackson (no relation). It illustrates the style of travel just described.

Fort Laramie was dubbed "Camp Sacrifice" because once many of the "overlanders" (a term coined to describe the emigrants), had reached this point of the trip, they started leaving things behind. There were no people to sell their surplus to because the other travelers had the same problem. Most people had simply brought too much. As a result the trail was littered with flour, bacon, clothing, and all other things imaginable. Traveling over the plains was much easier going than the rest of the trip. I imagine that when they arrived at Fort Laramie the mountains and desert were looming in their minds. What would make that trip easier? Less of a load to schlep to California or Oregon. Therefore, most emigrants purged their provisions before heading out from the fort. What they didn't leave by the side of the trail near Fort Laramie, they left later on as the Great Basin was crossed and the mountain peaks came into view.

Mr. Unruh wrote that "estimates of abandoned wagons on the 40 mile desert stretch (the Great Basin) ranged as high as

2,000 in 1850." He goes on to report that "one 1850 company found the regular trail so covered with dead and dying stock that they were compelled to forge a new trail."[8]

The pioneers relied on fresh water and various grasses. If they found such necessities, they were blessed. If not, they were cursed.

---

[8] Unruh, Jr., John, page 152.

CHAPTER THREE:
THE NATIVE AMERICANS

The Native Americans had traded with the
French and Canadian fur traders for years.
They were no strangers to White men and
women. The emigrants, on the other hand,
were fearful of the Native Americans. In the
early days of the Gold Rush, the Native
Americans were friendly, helpful, and good
trading partners. The Native Americans knew
their land and shared with the emigrants their
knowledge of the best routes to traverse, the
best water sources, be it rivers, streams, or
lakes. As the years went by, things
changed—and not for the better. William
Henry had positive relations with the Native
Americans he encountered. We know this
because of letters he wrote in 1850. At one
point, he wrote Sarah and told her he would
love to come back and bring the whole family.
He did not do this. Sarah was too afraid. And
as is the case with many a traveler, plans

changed.

The Native Americans became famous with the overlanders for stealing. They stole horses, oxen, liquor, and guns. The travelers became so used to the Native Americas and their stealing that the travelers thought of them as both dust and pesky mosquitoes. The Native Americans caused them worry but not enough to change their course to the west. Some did turn back, but most emigrants did not.

And while there were skirmishes where people died, these were isolated incidents. One of things I learned was that many ne'er-do-wells dressed up as Native Americans and terrorized the travelers. According to Mr. Unruh, these White men were the worst of the worst. They gave the Native Americans a bad name. And they scalped people. Again, though, this line of work as robbers and the like started out slow but then mushroomed into some well-known gangs during the 1850s. Guess they were the ones pictured on the WANTED posters that appeared in

Hollywood's rendition of life in the Wild West.

Circling the wagons, so to speak, I'd like to give a shout out to William Henry Dresser. In one letter he suggested that Sarah read an article published in The New York Tribune dated April 6, 1850 and written by the Honorable T. Butler King.[9] Mr. King wrote to the United States Secretary of State on March 22, 1850. Seems that Mr. King was sent by the President of the United States, Zachary Taylor to California via the Isthmus of Panama to ascertain how things were going in the far-off land of California. He did not mince words. Congress had not provided laws to govern the people who had traveled across the continent. As he put it, "They complained that the alcaldes, or judges, most of whom had been appointed or elected before the emigration had commenced were not lawyers by education or profession, and being Americans they were, of course, unacquainted with the

---

[9] T. Butler King, *New York Tribune*, April 6, 1850, page 4.

laws of Mexico, or the principles of civil law, of which they were founded."

To paraphrase... it was a legal mess.

Because, as Mr. King writes, "The sale of the territory by Mexico to the United States had necessarily cut off or dissolved the laws regulating the granting or procuring titles to land; and as our own land laws had not been extended over it, the people were compelled to receive such titles as were offered to them, without the means of ascertaining whether they were valid of not." This would affect William Henry and his sons and change the trajectory of their lives.

Mr. King goes on: "Towns and cities were springing into existence; many of them without legal rights to organize municipal authorities, or tax property or the citizens for the establishment of a police, the erection of prisons, or providing any of the means for the protection of life and property which are so necessary in all civil communities, and especially among a people mostly strangers to each other."

He then reports that the California population grew and so did trade with China, Chile, Mexico, and Australia. This led him to state, "California had, as it were by magic, become a State of great wealth and power."

What else could California do in that situation? It formed its own government. Some things never change. It is still a state of great wealth and power!

The issue of slavery was also addressed by our Mr. King. "Apparently and with great satisfaction, I am here to report that when California had their convention, of the 37 delegates to the convention, 16 were from slave holding states, 10 from non-slaving hold states, and 11 who were citizens of California under the Mexican government." And he reports, "It appears on the journal of the Convention that the clause in the constitution excluding slavery passed unanimously."

AND SO... The Honorable Mr. King's report was remarkable, well documented, and had the effect, once published in the New York Tribune of April 6, 1850, of influencing fence-sitters as well as eager beavers to "go for the gold" (so to speak). It certainly had that effect on my great-great-grandfather; thus he became the first generation of this branch of the Dresser family to go west to the land of mild weather, good soil, great mineral wealth, and the promise of prosperity.

Now you know the genesis of the Gold Rush trip insofar as William Henry Dresser was concerned. He was hooked. And because he was hooked, I became hooked and this led me to decide to take the trip he took. No covered wagon was involved. No oxen. This is 2023. Instead, with the idea of traveling in his footsteps, Rayman (my husband) and I headed back East to discover for ourselves what it was all about. Additionally, I will now relate his history and the history of the Dresser family to our own trip of discovery (including my version of what happened on our trip recently completed).

CHAPTER FOUR:
FOLLOWING THE TRAIL OF
WILLIAM HENRY DRESSER

Our train adventure began Friday, June 9, in
the afternoon. We were to embark at the
Portland, Oregon Train Depot. As we were
spending the summer in Portland, this was a
perfect train depot to catch the Empire
Builder train that ran from Portland, Oregon
to Chicago, Illinois. Additionally, we had
friends we planned to visit in Saint Paul,
Minnesota. This train trip made that possible.

This station is a grand old dame and a
perfect place to begin our trip to Saint Paul,
Minnesota. Having never been to that great

state, I'm tingling with excitement. Rayman on
the other hand, is worried about mosquitos in
the Land of 10,000 Lakes. I'm sure there are
other worries bouncing around in his
overactive mind, but today mosquitos were
mentioned.

Buzzing around my head is the family
history I've been researching.

To consider this information against my
own life: In my eleventh year, I had traveled
from Atascadero, California, to Paso
Robles—a car journey of about ten miles.
Added to that was a bus trip to Los Angeles at
some point. Oh, and trips to San Luis Obispo,
Morro Bay, and Cayucos, California (which
are all within the same county as Atascadero).
But that would be about it. Unworldly, I know.
It is instructive to me as I contemplate the
difference.

ALL ABOARD: JUNE 9, 2023

Today is our rendezvous with a train. We are scheduled for a 4:45 p.m. departure. It is now 6:00 p.m. and there is no train.

Where is that darn train? Well, let me back up and remind you, dear reader, what the plan was. We planned to depart Portland, Oregon (PDX) on train 28, The Empire Builder, to travel to Saint Paul, Minnesota. Additionally, we booked first class at the insistence of Rayman, who said something to the effect of, "I will not take a train if I can't have my own loo." To say he wasn't thrilled was an understatement. But Rayman is a fabulous person who knew he owed me a train trip. This has been an ongoing conversation for years... my begging and pleading to take Amtrak. Loving train travel, I was always suggesting train trips. Trains are comfortable and relaxing. No TSA, no lines, plenty of legroom.

Rayman, on the other hand, doesn't like Amtrak because it isn't a train you can count on. The following story is a case in point.

Which is unfortunate for me, since I'm the one who booked the trip!

So, where is that train?

Everything is so complicated. Our plan was to take Uber. I couldn't get the Uber app to work. Tamara, our daughter-in-law, luckily had come by for a glass of wine yesterday so she got the Uber booked for me. Well. Uber got canceled for the 4:45 train when we received word from Amtrak that the train would be leaving at 7:00 p.m. Then another alert from Amtrak came in. The all aboard time was now 9:00 p.m. Then the all aboard time became 10:00 p.m. So we got to thinking. Why don't we just drive down to the train depot and see if we can change our departure station to Vancouver, Washington, so the kids could take us to the train from their house (they live in Vancouver)?

On the way to the station to do just that, our son, Ryan, called us. He discovered the problem. The train had mechanical issues and that's why it was late. With that info percolating, we decided to go talk to a person—in person—at the train depot. That decision was made because yesterday when I had some software problems with the Amtrak website, I sat on hold waiting for a person from Amtrak to help me for like a hundred hours. The website's cute little "Just ask our digital assistant" didn't even work. Perhaps I should send Secretary Pete Buttigieg, head of the Dept. of Transportation, this epistle. Just sayin'.

Arriving at the train depot, I jumped out and sauntered into the station and met with a man I've named Archie. He said such classic things like, "Well, yes. Train travel is unpredictable." When I asked what the problem was, he told me, "Well, the train from Chicago broke down. A train to tow the train was dispatched. It is currently in Pasco, Washington, and it will arrive. Then we will change the engine and off it will go." And, when I asked him if the whole trip could be canceled, he said, "Excuse me while I take this call." Then he said to the person on the other end of the line, "Well, do you want to come in on track three or do you want another track?" This made me wonder if he ran everything at the train station. Holy mackerel.

When he finished his call, he said, "Now, what was your question?" I said, "I don't remember!" Really, people. I was now worried about who was in charge of things.

Then I piped up and asked, "Will the train be canceled?" He assured me it wouldn't because "he would know." OMG. Archie was to trains as Hal was to the space station.

Returning home, we drove over the Steel bridge. It is a drawbridge over the Willamette River. That caused me to remark that maybe we should have traveled by boat up the Columbia River.

It is now 1:15 a.m. We are sitting in the Metropolitan Lounge at the Portland train depot. To state the obvious, the train is still indisposed and Amtrak is holding us hostage. We spent $36 for a Lyft ride and the guy picked us up at 11:40 p.m. so we could get here on time. We could have walked here with no problem of missing this train.

My new friend, Archie, was still here at the depot. And he was still unsure about everything. Then we met some other new friends in the lounge. Their story was thus. They live in Portland but they booked the train to leave from Vancouver which was about a 15 minute trip by car so their daughter could take them to the Vancouver station (sound familiar?). Well, the Vancouver station closed at 9:30 p.m. leaving them on an outdoor bench, so they took the train coming from Seattle to Portland. And here they sit.

Finally, Archie came into the lounge and said all the sleepers could board. We were sleepers. We rose like a phoenix from the gray couch and headed for the door. When we got outside, Archie informed us there was a miscommunication and the train was, in fact, not ready after all. At this point the passengers started to get a bit rowdy until it was explained that a person had died on the train east of here. Then the train engine died west of Spokane. Then a rumor started that a wheel needed to be replaced along with the engine. Eye rolls were observed. But the death news did have a calming effect because really, how mad can you get when there is a death on a train?

Rayman mused aloud that we had booked the death train. Then we retreated to the lounge again and sat right back down on the gray sofa to continue the wait in comfort. Old train depots like this one provide fancy rooms for those traveling in first class. Soft sofas, hot coffee, cold beverages, a more private privy. These rooms are usually located away from the other travelers. It is akin to a first class lounge in an airport. Comes with the price of the ticket, I guess you could say.

Another few minutes dragged by and another employee came in and gave us our marching orders ... and to the train we went. This time it was the real deal. We boarded the sleeper car, the last car on the train and the last room on the car. The room we were assigned would have made a very good broom closet. But before complaining, we were extremely fortunate to have a window that looked out at the world as we lumbered by. I snapped a picture of a coal train that passed us and I affectionately named it The John Coltrain. Much of the trip this first morning ran along the Kootenai River. Not sure there was another way to see this part of the country except by train. The view from the train was extremely interesting.

If only you could have seen us at 3 a.m., trying to move into the room. Exhausted and annoyed, we threw stuff where it would fit... a six-inch wide closet, a chair in the corner, and hit the hay. My hitting the hay involved climbing up to the suspended bed without killing myself. And there I remained looking at the ceiling (which was about a foot from my nose). A suspended futon is a good descriptor of the contraption. And while I lay there being tossed around by the train, I held onto the thick cord that was attached in two places for the purpose of keeping me in my place. One roll in the wrong direction and I might have been the next person to die on this train.

A comparison. In 1849, William Henry's pillow was probably his trusty saddle. The ground was probably his bed. If it rained, he got soaked. Reminding myself of the hardships he endured altered my attitude and I turned toward the wall to count my blessings.

Rayman has been in a complete shock about the size of the room, the tardiness of the train, and without even saying it, I think I know this may be our last overnight train trip in the U.S.

Barring him throwing me, MaMa, from the train, we were on track to arrive in Saint Paul the next evening.

Slowly but surely, things improved. Our attitude adjustment was critical. Expectations were modified. Some examples. The second night, we slept head to toe on the lower bed that serves as a couch during the day. An employee came by and converted it to a bed, a single bed. This arrangement had the added benefit of not having constant air blaring at me from the ceiling vent (located right by my ear). I traded in the air-in-my-ear sensation for Rayman's feet-in-my armpit sensation.

The observation car was great. Chairs in various configurations tightly bolted to the floor sat in front of the windows on both sides of the car. Nice. Spent lots of time there. The dining car was well appointed sans crystal and silver or glass. Throwaway was the name of the game. At least they didn't use Styrofoam. And eating was family style, so we got to meet Harold and Maude. Just kidding … it was Harold and Margaret. He a professor from Connecticut, and she a resident of Spokane. Also in the dining car we met Tom and Claire. He a retired surgeon from Saint Paul, and she also from Saint Paul and intimated to be a doc but never stated it. They were a lovely couple returning from Glacier National Park. We traded info about our favorite websites for news and drinking spots in Saint Paul.

There was also a ninety-year-old woman who travels by the train almost constantly. She stopped by to tell me that this was the worst service she had ever experienced. She was traveling alone and could walk this tilting, lurching train better than myself. I almost fell into others' laps as I weaved down the aisle. She was sure-footed like a gecko. Oh, and she and another woman lodged their complaints with the person in charge of the entire train. That shocked me. Someone was in charge!

We had about five hours left before we arrived in Saint Paul. Because we were being picked up by friends, I sent out a warning that we were going to need showers. Yes, our cabin has a shower/toilet room but it was just too hard to stand and shower. Rayman decided to try and as he was trying to get in the door of the shower, the train lurched, which caused the door to slam shut and in doing so it knocked Rayman on his keester. Luckily he fell on the bed. So we scratched that plan and opted for a spits bath. Or was it a spitz bath? Whatever it was, it had to suffice. I'll just say this was the first time we had worn the same clothes for three days running. My linen overblouse and long skirt with no zipper or buttons was the perfect choice—although I did get my skirt caught in my undies and after strolling the train, someone told me about it. "Oh, quite the look!" I said as I pulled my skirt down. Then I thanked her. I just hoped I wasn't featured on TikTok. It may have gone viral.

The good news was that we arrived in one piece.

Day Three or Four or Five... good grief, I'm already confused!

For three days we took a time-out to visit our friends, Jim and Mari, whom we had met in New Zealand, ON A TRAIN! Our reunion was an opportunity to visit them in their habitat. Before we left their lovely White Bear Lake home, I rented a car via AutoSlash, a supposed money-saving app. Actually, the app saved us a lot of money and I highly recommend it. Example: first price was $2,200 for a SUV for a one way 12 day rental. Final price was $1,069. Anyway, we packed up our suitcases, loaded them into their car, and headed to an off-airport rental site for Hertz. It was conveniently located east around the bend, perhaps five miles.

There was only one problem. We missed the date of our reservation by showing up a day early. It was inexplicable, and yet it happened. Luckily Jim and Mari, our patient friends, had insisted on hanging around until we drove away. So, we sheepishly got back in the car and went back to their place for another evening. They were fabulous hosts. In many ways, they were like the pioneers.

People emigrating were very helpful to one another. If an axle broke, people would offer their help. If one group's food ran low, others would share their food if possible. Often the folks needing the help would pay for that help. Or people would trade with one another to help out those in need. I recall one story in one of the many books I read (For Further Reading, see the Bibliography at the back of this book) that described flour as being the only thing left that the members of a particular party could share. This implies that flour and water became a meal. It was that bad. Scurvy, a condition caused by a lack of vitamin C as a result of not eating enough fruit and vegetables, was a result for many who ran out of all food excepting flour on route to California. Sagebrush, Nevada's state flower, gives you some idea of why scurvy was a problem. Livestock wouldn't even eat it because of its bitter and pungent taste. People and livestock were in full agreement about sagebrush.

Back to the trip. Next morning, off we went again to the Hertz rental office. This time, the car was there. A black Rogue with 35,000 miles on it. We figured this Rogue had been rode hard and put away wet; it had a rear gate that only opened when it wanted to and lacked the safety features we love, like a lane-changing warning which alerts the driver to the danger of being killed.

Assured of a departure, Jim and Mari took their leave.

Our Rogue was not a covered wagon. It was not so crammed full of provisions that we had to buy some mules to drag it while we walked along beside it. So, travel puts things into perspective, if nothing else.

FIRST STOP, BELOIT!
June 15th, 2023

Beloit, Wisconsin. This is where my great-great-grandparents lived in the 1840s and 1850s.

Beloit is now a small city with a population of 37,000 that runs together with many other nearby small cities in Wisconsin and Illinois. Before we arrived in Beloit, Roscoe and other neighboring towns, I had arranged an appointment with a woman at the historical society, or the library, or both. It was a bit confusing but the lady was clear about history, so it was a worthwhile appointment.

It is a very sad fact that women go missing in historical records. Given this situation, my trip to Roscoe and Beloit was very disappointing. My great-great-grandmother was a member of the Jenks family. The Jenks family was an old, prominent family in the area. And yet, Sarah Jenks Dresser, who had lived and died here, could not be found in any records. In a tour of the cemetery today, we inspected many Jenks markers. She wasn't there, either. Cremation did not become a "thing" practiced by Europeans in North America until 1876 according to the website, Smart Cremation. Sarah's remains are still an unsolved mystery.

Fun fact. Sarah's parents owned several pieces of land. One large parcel currently hosts a freeway interchange. Another parcel is dotted with homes.

The other news of the day is that we got lost. Shocking, I know. We were as hungry as two rattlesnakes as we slithered into the car and headed to Bananas and Cherries, a bakery not too far away. (We have been relying on Waze, the GPS app, to find our way for us.) When we arrived at the bakery, Rayman said, "They look closed." This was funny because we had an experience once when looking for another restaurant and when we arrived, the sign in the window said, CLOSED ON TUESDAYS. It was a Tuesday. And for years this has been a running joke. It turns out many restaurants close on Tuesdays.

Flash forward to today, June 16. The bakery was closed and there was a sign. CLOSED ON THURSDAYS. There were other cars arriving at the same time. We rolled down our window and asked the driver of one car if the place was any good. She was very enthusiastic in her recommendation and then she said, "But I didn't know they closed on Thursday."

Waze was consulted after I Yelped for another place to eat. Our second selection was Alpha Bakery. So off we went. Only the road leading to the road we needed was closed completely. We reasoned that if we turned around and went down one block or two, we would find Alpha Bakery. No. Railroad tracks were running through the neighborhood, requiring a big detour. So, we gave up on that restaurant. What were the chances?

We ended up driving to Beloit and ate at a place called Bushel and Pecks. It was fabulous. An interesting observation here. Restaurants include bakeries, groceries, and the like in many the same storefront; a concept of which we both approve because of the convenience it offers. And another general observation is that things are clean here, like the rest stops. Spotless. Oh, and there are a lot of police in these parts. City police and highway patrol officers roam around and park behind bushes with their radars pointing here and there.

June 17: From here to there

My mind keeps returning to dear Sarah. I
am including here a letter that she wrote to
William as he was either telling his patrons to
smile for the camera or to open wide for the
tooth extraction.

Beloit Nov 14, 1847

My dear William

yours of Nov. 6 I received on the 9 and the one you wrote 28 the
money came safe that you speak of Mr Wadswort thought we had
better wait a few days and he woo have a good chance to send your
things for them by private coveyance to you the man did not come
as soon he expected James was here last Friday and said if they
had not gone he would send them by on the stage I should have
written before but I supposed your things ware sent last Tuesday
or wednesy day.James said he would write a few lines to you I
suppose he told you we are well and we still enjoy good health for
us and am glad to hear that you enjoy the same great Blessing
since I wrote to you last I have had a great deal of trouble with
old Temp they have been takeing up some of the bridge and fixing
it over and put old Temp all out of a fix—she was gone five or
six milkings at one time we do not have her half of the time.
Albert is of a hunting for her now. I am a fraid she will go dry
unless we have a place to shut her up and feed her hay I want you
should tell me what to do with the old sow for she torments me so that
I can not see straight some one has been so good as to take down
the pen you built for her the boys say it was Mr Hance and I have
no place to put her—if I had my way about it I would put her in
the pork Barrel James thinks so to I am afraid if we dont some
of our neighbours will do it for us she troubles them so. Mr. Hills
says he will take her and let you have pork for her now, he says
that his hogs are as heavy as she is James says she is the fattest
he ever saw her James has not killed that pig for me yet. I do not
know when he will he is drove knight and day in his shop, I have
got that from Culbert on Hacke Store I got some cloth for the boys
close. I had to give more than I expected for it I took it all up
and had to take some money to get the boys Caps I told them maby
pa would scold—they said he would not, Aby says Pa will be real
glad that ma has got them some Caps now they can go to meating and
sunday School The baby is as proud with his new bonet as pa is
with his new vest but he would be prouder still if he could see pa
and give him a good sweet kiss on his forehead he would make it all
ring, maryett says tell William that she is sitting in the big chair
by the stove a rocking the baby in the cradle, Angeline was here

the next day after I got your letter says if you will send her a
letter she will answer it. Mother has gone gone home. Mr Hance
and family are well our quartley meeting is yesterday and today,
wood is very high James thinks I had better get my wood by the
load and get it chopped James got that money of Dan that is all
I have got by me, I have got to have some wood soon, James has
not got any grain for me excepting a half bushel of Corn He has
not got grain he expected. Mr Hance will take that shoat or get
some one else to take it, O I have got me a new dress, cheap at
that some like the old woman Coprus and white, tu and tu I do
not know of anything new to write only they say Emely North is a
going to be marries to Orrin Cros'sman, Albert thinks it would be
hard to live without pa I will not say what I think about it
this time I want you to write and tell me what to do and how to
do and how you are a going to get your shirts or a sly when you
are comeing home—if I could see you I could talk faster than I
can write I have not got my Carpet yarn yet I must quit.

               I remain your ever afectionate wife

                                   Sarah Dresser

I believe I have done everything you wanted I should do

To   Postmark: None
     Mr William Desser
     Madison   Postage: None
     Dane Co
     W T

    The letter goes on, but this page illustrates
how life was for her, holding down the farm
and taking care of the children. She was not a
withering flower but a woman to be reckoned
with and quite up to the task with help from
friends, neighbors, and her nearby family.

    After our interesting visit to Beloit and

Roscoe, we jumped in the Rogue, and hightailed it to our next planned stop, Fort Madison.

FORT MADISON

Fort Madison sits on the Mississippi River and our hotel sports a view of the river. We got a great deal on a room with a view. Ain't that great? Well, there were a couple of problems we were unaware of when we booked the room. Between us and the river there are railroad tracks and they are very busy and the trains coming and going blast their horns. The days of train whistles are over. These horns would wake the dead. But fear not. The room came with two sets of earplugs.

The other problem is the sad fact that this town is dying. We sauntered about looking for a restaurant. The Kingsley Hotel lady, who was dressed in an interesting outfit (which may have included a tutu), recommended a joint a couple of doors down. We walked by and there was not one patron in the place at dinnertime so we kept walking. There were closed-up shops and when I say closed up, I mean out of business, caput. There's a prison up the hill and we met a man in the bar of the hotel who had retired from the joint. Other than the prison, the hotel and fort, there's not much here. We kept walking.

A few blocks down the road we discovered a grocery store that was still in operation and so we inquired within. "Nope. There's really no place to eat here. You'd need to drive for miles for a meal." This is what the cashier told us. With that advice, we strolled back to the Kingsley Hotel and raided our own room for snacks. And that was our dinner.

Incidentally, our hotel was built in the late 1800s. It was very cool. The snacks were courtesy of our friends, Mari and Jim of White Bear Lake, Minnesota. They saved us from the pangs of hunger.

The road trip to Fort Madison involved all backroads where we saw more corn than we had ever seen before. Mile after mile after mile of young corn stalks reaching for the sun. We were also amazed at how many roads in Iowa, Nebraska, and Wyoming have more farm implements rolling along than, say, cars or trucks. As Californians, we became despondent that all those years spent in traffic jams could have been avoided if our federal taxes had been used to improve our infrastructure instead of in places like Iowa, which simply didn't need all those paved roads they paved. In an effort of full disclosure: our backroads trip did involve one stretch of gravel road. Chuck Grassley, Iowa's current senior sitting Senator should investigate.

On the previous page is a picture of Fort Madison, a reproduction. Like many forts built in the 1800s, it sustained damage by fire, flood, and other calamities. The history buffs have replaced and rebuilt parts of the fort. From 1804 to 1813 the original fort stood until the Army abandoned it after it was burned to the ground by the Army troops as they left. Only the chimneys remained. The fort had been under siege by the Sauk Indians, who resented that the fort was essentially interrupting their trade routes. An interesting aside, the penitentiary in Fort Madison used its inmates for much of the work on the restoration of the fort in the 1980s.

MOVING ALONG TO NAUVOO AND THE MORMON TRAIL

While we were driving the backroads, I noted that William Henry followed the Rock River, the closest river to his home in Beloit. The Rock (as the locals call it now) was an obvious choice because it flowed southwest, the direction he was heading. We followed the Mississippi because I was enamored with Old Man River and there were roads that hugged its banks. The only disappointment? The huge silos and related factories impeding the view.

Our plan was to follow the Mormon trail after first visiting Nauvoo, Illinois. For those not familiar with Nauvoo, it was the settlement the Mormons, under the leadership of Joseph Smith, built and then occupied before heading to Salt Lake City. This religious sect had been persecuted in the east and so they covered their wagons and headed west.

Today, Nauvoo was mostly quiet until we took a street that led to a statue of Dear Leader. There we discovered a crowd of people all dressed as though it was still 1840-something. Long pastel dresses for the young girls, white shirts and ties for the young boys. They frolicked around in the dust doing old-fashioned dances. The only thing that came close to matching this vision of living in the past was when we were driving Highway 2 and came across an Amish horse and buggy trotting along on the highway.

It's all ears. That is what Iowa is… a state of ears of corn. Hundreds of miles of rolling hills planted in corn. I could also characterize Iowa as the roller-coaster state. The highways go up to the top of hills before they head down the other side of the hills. Quite fun, actually. All it lacked were Burma Shave signs. Here is an old Burma Shave adage for you.

> ## CATTLE CROSSING
> ## PLEASE DRIVE SLOW
> ## THAT OLD BULL
> ## IS SOME COW'S BEAU

In 1850 my great-great-grandfather crossed this land in his covered wagon and spoke fondly of it, although he did mention in a letter written from Kelsey's Diggings near Coloma, California, dated October 13, 1850 (after his trip had ended) that "With respect to my Exodus across the wilderness (falsely called the Plains for that term is only applicable to the valley of the Platt)...." The plains were easily traversed compared to the Rockies/Sierra Nevada ranges and I suppose the Great Basin. I say I suppose because he did not write while traversing that portion of the trip. That was probably because, as he explained in the same letter, "I had not a single hours leisure for 72 days, each morning up at 3 and about 10 to bed at night, since my arrival I have gained flesh and fatter now than you ever saw me my weight is about 158."[10]

Nota Bene: I took literary license and corrected some of the spelling and punctuation to make reading easier. While this is true history, I elected to at least make it more easily read.

Envisioning William Henry moving across Iowa in 1850 almost defies imagination because today it looks much different with miles and miles of corn. The land then was treed and covered in native grasses. A machete may have been involved.

To reach Nauvoo we traversed a toll bridge that spanned the Mississippi. To leave Nauvoo, we took another free bridge across the Mississippi. We were starving. It was about 10:30 a.m. and food was in order. We stopped

---

[10] From page 23 of copies from Bancroft Library.

at a dive, I mean a greasy spoon cafe and had a good breakfast. Then we took on the rolling hills by heading to Cordyn, Iowa, which was a few hours away and very close to the Missouri border. We did this because my great-great-grandparents on my **dad's** side of the family were thought to be buried there. This endeavor turned out to be much more complicated for a variety of reasons and we were unsuccessful in our mission to visit their graves.

We did, however, visit the Prairie Trails Museum in Cordyn and met Dixie. She was delightful and helped us search for gravesites and Thomas (my maiden name) artifacts. Another trip will be needed to finish my research on my dear relatives. It was getting late and we needed to move along because we had to get to Council Bluffs before every deer in Iowa threw itself in front of our car at dusk.

As a detour in the story, when we drove from White Bear Lake in Minnesota to Beloit, Wisconsin, we saw dead deer every few miles. The roads are lined in big, green, leafy trees and the deer were not easy to spot unless they were sprawled dead on the road. It was deer carnage.

But back to Iowa.

The reason I wanted to go to Council Bluffs is because William wrote about it. Of course, Council Bluffs now is a thriving metropolis of 62,000 plus people and sits on Iowa's western state line across from Omaha, Nebraska. Being a native Californian, the idea of driving the full length or width of an entire state is almost a foreign idea. It takes days to drive the 760 miles of California and if you are a lover of views, it takes longer, much longer. If you are in the Los Angeles basin or the Bay Area, it takes even more time. As far as the width, it is possible here and there. On average California is 250 miles across. Iowa, as a comparison, a state that is 199 miles long and 310 miles wide, is doable—although your gluteus maximus might remind you of your silliness.

Here I include a copy of a letter William Henry wrote to a Mr. C.W. Haskins. Mr.

Haskins was the author of *The Argonauts of California*. See below.

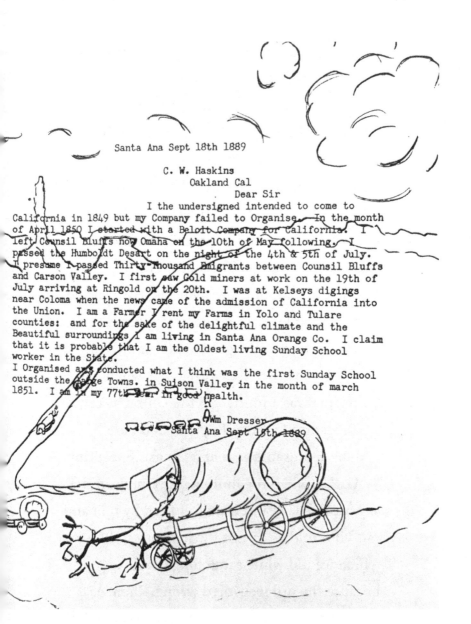

Santa Ana Sept 18th 1889

C. W. Haskins
Oakland Cal
Dear Sir

I the undersigned intended to come to California in 1849 but my Company failed to Organise. In the month of April 1850 I started with a Beloit Company for California. I left Counsil Bluffs now Omaha on the 10th of May following. I passed the Humboldt Desart on the night of the 4th & 5th of July. I presume I passed Thirty Thousand Emigrants between Counsil Bluffs and Carson Valley. I first saw Gold miners at work on the 19th of July arriving at Ringold on the 20th. I was at Kelseys digings near Coloma when the news came of the admission of California into the Union. I am a Farmer I rent my Farms in Yolo and Tulare counties: and for the sake of the delightful climate and the Beautiful surroundings I am living in Santa Ana Orange Co. I claim that it is probable that I am the Oldest living Sunday School worker in the State.

I Organised and conducted what I think was the first Sunday School outside the large Towns. in Suison Valley in the month of march 1851. I am in my 77th year in good health.

Wm Dressen
Santa Ana Sept 18th 1889

Notice that this letter was written in Santa

Ana, California, in 1889 when William Henry was 76 years old. And it was typed. Typewriters were just coming into use in the late 1800s. I would love to know about his typewriter, but alas, it remains a mystery. The important point here is that he mentions Council Bluffs; he tells Mr. Haskins that he intended to leave for California in 1849 but the trip fell through. This adds critical information about his early plans. He yearned to go west at least a year before he actually did. And he arrived at the gold fields on July 19, 1850. He was at Kelsey's Diggings when California was admitted to the Union in 1850.

Presently, this trip Rayman and I are making represents ease at its finest. Excepting yesterday, when the fluffy white clouds in the sky turned dark and were followed by rain and our GPS told us to exit the highway right, which we did while scratching our heads because the order seemed wrong. Then we headed down a road and when the GPS— let's start calling it Rover—told us to turn on a dirt road to nowhere, we knew something was amiss. With lightning in the distance, perhaps the signal to Rover malfunctioned. Comparing that to a rainstorm in a covered wagon or on horseback, it became obvious that our situation was a big nothing burger.

A thought. Perhaps we would all be better off if we would just stop and reflect on our easy lives on occasions like this. No dead oxen, no ruts to endure, rest stops for necessary business. We live in the lap of luxury these days (except for global warming and other ills).

On the next page is a copy of the transcribed letter that William wrote from the Council Bluffs.

Kaynesville, May 1st/50

My Dear Sarah

I fear you will think my delay rather long before you receive
this, I have had nothing of importance to write. When we arrived
at Monro I Bot half of N Otis team and all that appertained
theireto, one fourth of all the provisions tent, stove, cooking
utensils etc that Fargo, Carter & Otis had I paid him (Otis) One
hundred and five Dollars cash, twelve Dollars in dried meat, and
gave him my note for forty seven Dollars more than for the cash
expenses and the price of another horse I shall be still indebted
to him, whatever the establishment will fitch will help pay back
this outfit, we now expect that it will be occonemey prity soon
after crosing the Rocky Mountains to throw away our waggon and
pack through there being a nearer rout discovered by the Mormans
last fall which can be packed a little more than half the time
that waggons can pas the other road if I had known before I had
started what I now know I should come here by water bot 2
horses and packed all the way I might of stayed at home 3 weeks
longer; in fact comeing as we did we would have done better to
have stayed at home ten days longer, people were not only crazy
mad but were fools at that for they would not proffit by
experience, we very soon found that we were to early and we fooled
away most of the seccond. week, and now we are altogether to early,
we got here some 5 hours over 3 week from the time we started we
shall hardly leave here before the first of next week, the wither
is very cold water fros in the pail last night more than 1/2 inch
thick, there is scarce any grass at all in the Sloughs about enough
on the dry prairie to pasture goats I don't know that I ever saw the
grass [   ] forward on the Rolling than the wet prairie, nearly
all through Iowa the land is similiar to De'Kalb Co Ill   the
greatest [expectation] is that it is more Rolling, the Prairies are
very rich and emencly large the distance from Beloit here is 470
for near the last 300 miles there was a very sparce settlement
quite lattey settled (about 3 years) without grain or hay we had
to lay in our grain and hall it the whol of that distance without
hay for our horses, of course our horses lost considerable flesh,
we only past 4 dead horses we pased the grave of one man from
Racine and heard of the death of one from Belvidere the former
caught cold which terminated in inflamation on the Longues the
other sleeping in his waggon a cold rain fell on his head which
induced inflamation in the head—those who started so early were
much more exposed than we have been twice there has been rain
enough to lay the dust and that is all, if we could only have a
good rain and terminate warm we should have grass very soon—If we
don't have rain within 2 or 3 weeks we shalnot have the pleasure of

a good drenching until we catch it from the winter rains in the
diggins for we are informed that scarce ever rains on the plains
or in fact on the whole rout after leaving here a week or 2 or 3.
I have had conversations with several who have past and repast
the whole distance and I cant find anything to dread, any great
hardships to encounter, I have enquired much for the most
dificult things that we have to encounter and am not able to find
what they are, we meet with meny women and children with happy
and bouyant harts bound for Cal$ and Origon, with refference to
Cal$ our health, ultimate success, and everything pertaing to our
great enterpris I wish you would obtain Hon T. Butler King's
Report on Calafornia to J. M. Clayton Secy of State and read it
and then do as I did studyit all over the second time, excepting
that part (the introduction) pertaining to the state Government,
you will find it in the N. Y. Tribune of Apr. 6 or many other
subsequent papers, we have had no sickness among us and the
emigration as far as I can learn is very healthy, some 3 or 4 have
had the small pox but it has been so light that some dispute its
being small pox but it is small pox no doubt some few dayes we
had to cross a good many sloughs otherwayes the roads were as good
as roads could well be many not accoustome to them some mired the
horses and broke there waggons but Otis & I have not broke the
first thing neither have our horses been sick. We are told that
we shall be obliged to keep a strict watch every night to keep the
Indians from stealing horses beyond that we have nothing to fear I
wish you [could] send a doller to Br Adams the Methodist preacher
I mean the.painter for my dues to the S. of Tempeence if you
don't hear anything to the contrary 3 months hence send one
doller more. Mills gave you three Dollars I presume that I gave
him for you, you have probably got the auger and draw knife from
Clements the Gouldsmith and the chisels from Lancaster, Cemera
did not pay that fifteen dollars as he agreed the buisness is all
at Br Easterly cousin friend Mills to see to that for you,
Healy told me that he would pay George out of the store or any
other way enytime some ten Dollars; I would say that I forgot to
pay my dues to the Sons,—And when I wrote to James I forgot to tell
him about Saxby, Old Downer is witness to the bargain and B
Hackett & Drake heard him agree to meet me at there rooms to do the
work at three o'clk the friday previous to my departure which he
neglected to do so I filled my part of the Contract Hackett sayed
that Sacksby could not enforce payment I dont know when I shall
write to James again please transcribe what I have writen about
this affair & what ever would be interesting in this letter to him—
I left that French buisnes with he had a clame of $2.00 When he
collects it from French he will be entitled to 3 Dollers more
$5.00. I gave the butcher a chance in for about $4.00 & Dexter $3
more makeing in all $12 now if this is ever got and you could get
the ballance (which is rather doubtfull) there would be some $15
for you, trying will cast nothing stick to it and keep trying, if

a judgement is obtained rather than let others get hold of it lit
him satisfy the above claimes then perhaps by throwing of a quarter
he would be induced to pay directly to you now these fellows will
be on the allert and will surely catch French and get a judgement,
the trick will be to get the rest yourself As to the enterprise in
which we are engaged there is everything to encourage and nothing
to discourage in the common course of human events, after much
inquiry I find that the only great dificulty that I had to
encounter was <u>surmounted</u> when friend George with that true
generosaty found only in a true and humble heart (may God grant
that I may be enabled to reciprocate the favour) lent me that money—
I shall not write until just before we leave — There can hardly be
said to be any town at the Bluffs this is a Mean Mormon Hole 8
miles from one fery some 6 stores & a host of Helleryes filled
with beastly drunkenness May 9th We are now on the Banks of the
river of Mud (Missourie) we have left the Beloit Co (i e Fargo,
Carter, Otis & myself' for the purpose of goin with Mr Hicks of
Elkhorn Walworth Co Wis who has just returned got his wife and
returning you can gudge of the dreadfull hardships I have seen
several men returning to Cal with their wives my only wish is that
you and the children were with me,we cross today expecting to leave in
a day or two Cap' Hicks sayes he will put us through in 70 dayes.
Emediatly on the receipt of this write to San Francisco We have
Bot a horse pritty good for $40. We found one spot of <u>good grass</u>
last 4 dayes horses done well I shall write from Salt Lake,and now
I want to say something to my Boyes t'el Albert & Charley not to
forget Pa and Love one another I am writing in the waggon with
hundreds around me and my eyes forbid me writing mutch tel Lanney to
give Tilley a good kiss for Pa, Give my respects to All and believe me

Your affectionate husband
Wm Dresser

P S

    Get some one to get our letters from the Methodist Church and
attach to Roscoe I intended to get my letter but forgot it pray
for me and yourself and children and I will do the same every day
that God may grant that we may yet enjoy each others company untill
we are taken hence

      W D

Addressed to: Postmark: Nebraska Iowa May 13

    Mrs Sarah Dresser   Postage: 10¢
    Roscoe Winnebago Ill

COUNCIL BLUFFS AND OMAHA

Council Bluffs was yet to be explored by us. We booked a Best Western sight unseen; when I called the hotel the woman told me it was not close to the freeway. When we arrived at our Best Western, the most expensive hotel thus far, the reception desk recommended a place called Salty Dogs for dinner. It was within walking distance. We really wanted to avoid driving again so we walked around the corner and discovered the hotel was situated behind a huge Pilot gas station/truck stop. And the trucks were all parked and running, releasing a ghastly amount of diesel fumes into the atmosphere. Because we were hermetically sealed inside the hotel (couldn't open the windows), we beat most of the fumes. It was, however, not Shangri-La.

For William Henry the most noxious fumes he suffered were the odors emanating from the rotting livestock along the trail. At least rotting animals were biodegradable. While he did not pontificate about rotting animals, other letter writers did. Below is a passage.

Arriving at a spot in the journey, a mirage appeared. Mr. Bruff explains.[11]

"Oxen had stampeded for it, hoping to quench their burning thirst, and left their swelled-up carcasses over the plain in that direction, as far as we could discern them. Passed since noon-halt [lunch] not counting those just mentioned, to the South, 103 dead oxen, 3 do horses, and 1 mule. Saw also 3 abandoned oxen, lying down, anxiously looking back on the road, in vain, for succor from suffering and a slow death.—One of these nearest to the road, I shot, terminating its sufferings.—The wolves tonight will finish the others."

By the way, the Salty Dogs restaurant was a bust for us. Wings were their specialty. We ordered a hamburger but I don't know if Rayman enjoyed his half because I could not hear him. The decibels were only exceeded by

---

[11] Bruff, p. 151

the tattoos in the joint. Oh, well. The location was well situated.

Also, worth mentioning. It was the weekend of the big national college baseball tourney held in Omaha every year. In this regard our timing was off. We paid three times the normal rate for our room. Supply and demand, baby.

That was the end of travel for the day. On to Nebraska tomorrow.

NEBRASKA, JUNE 18TH

A day of travel on fairly busy roads began with a cup of ice cream at Costco in Omaha followed by a fig bar in the car. We needed gas and Costco had been our go-to stop for gasoline when there was one nearby. If retail therapy was needed, well, Costco was good for that too.

William Henry's retail therapy was satisfied by trading for things like horses, oxen, mules. Overlanders traded with Native Americans. They traded with fellow travelers. And they purchased things from each other as well. Need an axle? Hit up a stranger or better yet, find a deserted wagon on the trail. Of course, this wasn't always possible. Many travelers abandoned their wagons and went by horse or on foot. Or they joined up with other wagon trains if the other travelers would have them. Sore at themselves for having spent the money for a wagon, some would tear the wagon apart and set it on fire. Brotherly love, not. Presumably, they would then resume the journey on foot or horseback.

Nebraska's highways were flat going east to west and up and down going south to north. Mostly we went west. A few observations. People drove fast on two-lane roads and the speed limit was sixty-five on those two-lane roads. What could go wrong? Squished like a bug if a wrong move is made. We arrived in Cozad, Nebraska, about 4 p.m. and called it quits for the day. Did some laundry and went to dinner.

There were many Mexican restaurants located in the small towns. We dined at one that had an elephant out in front. To the casual person, this might elicit a surprise. However, "seeing the elephant" was a term that emigrants used while traveling. If I infer it correctly, it meant finding what they were looking for. However as the early overlanders traveled, the elephant sighting may have referred to bad things that happened.

Travel for the Dresser party might have been a bit easier through Nebraska because the

Mormon Trail was a fairly straight trail thanks to nature's engineers, the buffalo, and the elk. The Native Americans who had traversed the plains for centuries followed the buffalo and the elk. The route was observable and well known. Native grasses provided food for the livestock. The Platte River ran the length of the route in Nebraska, providing needed water for the pioneers' trek.

Fun fact. Nebraska was the only territory admitted to the Union over a presidential veto. Slavery was the issue. As a result, Nebraska entered into the United States late in the game after the Civil War in 1867. To read more about this matter of considerable interest, aim your browser at the following:

history.nebraska.gov/nebraska-statehood-launched-in-troubled-times

Another fact from the website states, "By 1867 the Civil War had decided the fate of slavery and the problem of the day was whether the newly freed people were to be granted the right to vote. The Nebraska constitution originally submitted to Congress, in common with the constitutions of most other northern states, restricted the right to vote to white males. Women were not considered qualified to vote."

We have indeed come some distance to form a more perfect union. As the old Virginia Slims cigarette ad proclaimed to women in the 1970s, "You've come a long way, baby."

But I digress.

With speed limits on my mind, I considered the trip in 1850 again. It was slow and tedious. A company had a good day if it made twenty-four miles...this according to Mr. Bruff's accounts. He diligently noted the weather, the pace of travel, all the grave markers, and he counted the dead animals. His account was to the Gold Rush what I think Lewis and Clarks' notes were to the crossing of the continent in 1804. Bruff's drawings captured the topography beautifully. Quite a book and a great resource for travelers interested in history.

IN A RUT AND OUT OF A RUT

Today, June 19, we were challenged to find those old, elusive wagon wheel ruts. We started the day in Cozad, which is somewhat famous because it is located on the 100th meridian of the Earth. Once we drove under the sign that straddled the highway, we were officially in the western United States (contiguous, that is). This felt like a slight accomplishment.

Our attention then turned to finding those ruts, some of which may have been from the wagon William Henry drove. That specificity cannot be verified—but I can dream. After consulting the National Park Service app and the road atlas that has been living between the Rogue's console and the passenger seat (a bit ragged at this point), I was lost in the fog of confusion. But we persevered.

We snapped this picture to show the depths we were going to in order to see the ruts. This cornfield is on the private property we entered (trespassed?) during our search. No ruts were

observed and we weren't shot, so it was good-
good.

The Nebraska highway was littered with
Historical Markers that featured information
about the emigrants, mostly Mormon, who
crossed the continent. Going sixty-five mph
made it a bit difficult to notice them in time to
stop, but we managed... often in a cloud of
dust before we came to a halt. So did other
travelers manage to stop and we met and
talked with them. In this manner we were

given directions to various spots to explore. It occurred to me that this is also what the emigrants did. The wagon trains were often situated near each other both for a nooner (the word "nooner" was used in a sentence back then as such: "We nooned in this spot by the river and after a lunch of hard bread and coffee, we moved on." Or "While nooning or at day's end, emigrants camping nearby were a constant source of information and disinformation." Although Rayman and I weren't nooning, we were visiting like the emigrants did: to collect information about the area's history and about the way we were headed down the highway. This is how we discovered Windlass Hill.

In the past, a windlass was a "thing." This was news to us. It aided in traversing steep descents that they came upon during the journey. One of the first uses documented was at Windlass Hill. Here are a few pictures we snapped. At our age it was a climb to ascend the hill the pioneers descended but somehow we made it. I was on high alert because a sign said it was rattlesnake habitat. Rattlers were mentioned often in the Bruff book. This looked like a perfect snake habitat to me. With fear in my heart, I plodded up the hill in shoes that were woefully inadequate. It was over ninety degrees and we did a bit of huffing and puffing.

I had read that ruts were located in various areas, some of which were not near a road. We elected to find a rut near a road, which was a dandy. See the previous page.

When we completed the hike, we stopped at a rural gas station/restaurant/convenience store and bought an extra-big bottle of cold Gatorade and shared it. It was gone in about three miles. All of it. Then we took time to reflect on what we had seen.

When one drinks Gatorade, one does not need to worry about contracting cholera from the beverage. The pioneers only had streams, creeks, rivers, rivulets, waterfalls and lakes, from which to drink. If they drank bad water, it killed them. If their animals drank bad water, it would likely kill them too. As you've read several times already, dead animals littered the trails. Every day the pioneers came upon oxen, mules, and horses that were either dead or dying. Some almost-dead animals were shot and eaten (as previously mentioned).

Before we climbed Windlass Hill, we had

stopped at the Lincoln County Historical Museum on Buffalo Bill Road and met a woman named Jeanie. We also met a former DEA agent who was a railroad train connoisseur of some renown. Our conversation was brisk, teeming with information of railroad trains and emigrants. What these historical societies and museums had to offer was impressive. For instance, we learned that during WWII, women for miles around North Platte organized to provide food to every single military person arriving by train. North Platte may have had the world's largest train yard. According to the *Guinness Book of World Records*, "The largest rail freight yard is Bailey Yard in North Platte, Nebraska, USA. Operated by the Union Pacific Railroad, it has a total length of 12.8 km (8 miles) and covers an area of 11.5 km² (2,850 acres)." This honor was bestowed in 2014 so presumably it was very large in the 1940s. Every soldier heading east or west who arrived there received food provided by these wonderful people. The history was astounding. Here is a link to learn more about this community effort.

lincolncountymuseum.org/3-volunteering-at-the-canteen

I made an effort to support these museums and historical societies, so now I am a proud owner of a Canteen T-shirt and tickets to a raffle for a quilt. It was the least I could do. That all happened before the hill climb, which was a good thing. After the hill climb, we might not have stopped to visit the museum.

Where was William in this area of the country? Letters from him became less frequent. Fort Laramie was the next stop where he paused and composed a letter to Sarah. He sounds downright chipper, which amazes me. I feel like he fared much better than many people described in *The Plains Across*, a thoroughly documented book. See Bibliography.

One of the great landmarks on the trail was Independence Rock. It could be seen by the emigrants from thirty miles away. By 1850, it was one crucial rock formation that the emigrants longed to see. We stopped by the visitor's center and were wowed by the art there. After purchasing a book about women in the Gold Rush, we headed to the town of Scottsbluff. After dinner, we retired and I blogged about the events of the day.

SCOTTSBLUFF, JUNE 19

Today, we spent the whole day in
Scottsbluff, Nebraska, which was located near
Independence Rock and Scott's Bluff and we
were certainly happy about that. After
breakfast, we headed out to Scott's Bluff,
which was designated a National Monument
and managed by the U.S. Parks Service. On the
way there, we visited The Legacy of the Plains
Museum. The building was abuzz with women
"hookers," according to our guide. She was a
mischievous local woman. When she said they
were hookers, she blushed. Hookers were the
women who made rugs. And we were very
happy to have arrived that day because there
was an exhibit of hand-hooked rugs to admire.
They were fabulous.

There was also a room of women quilters.
Only one quilt was on display.

The museum supplied information of all
sorts, including stories about the pioneers who
traveled through this area. William was one of
those pioneers and it was a thrill to know that

I may have walked the ground he did. The ground I speak of is the entire area surrounding the bluff.

How did the bluff get its name? As the story goes, one Mr. Scott became ill in the area and so his friends left him to die alone. When they returned the following year, they found his remains and thereby named the bluff Scott's Bluff after their friend.

After leaving the museum, we used our Senior Park Pass to enter the monument. Unbeknownst to us, the bluff had a road winding up to the top that allowed people in cars to reach the apex of the monument. The road with many tunnels was constructed during the Great Depression by the government to counter the sky-high unemployment by providing needed employment so people could afford food and shelter.

Not knowing what we would find, we followed our noses to the top of this sandstone and ash structure, which has continued to erode from the wind and elements that blow almost continuously in this area. Seeing tunnels cut through sandstone was a surprise. When I asked the ranger about the project, he was of the opinion that this road would not be possible today. Sandstone is as the name implies, sand. The Environmental Protection Agency might object to such a project today. This, of course, is conjecture.

Be that as it may, the road was a thrill and gave us a bird's-eye view of the terrain. William describes the bluff in his Fort Laramie letter of May 1850.

Fort Laramie May 29/50

Dear Sarah

It is with pleasure that I have an oportunity to write to you
although it is imposable to say when you will receive this as it
will not leave this place until the return mail from the Bluffs to
Salt Lake passes here, which left that place (the Bluffs) ten
dayes before we did. I feel thankfull to the Allwise Providence
that my health is as good as I could wish and well it might for a
healthier country than this place to the Missourie the Sun neaver
shone on. no accident as happened to us man or beast except one
man's horse got to wheat (feed) in the night and eat so much that
he kit the bucket. The season thus far is very backward, the grass
did not furnish a good bite untill we came on the North branch of
the Platt on the 23rd then we enjoyed the lucsury of some Glorious
Showers, and two tremendous blows the rest of the time greatly to
my surprise the rest of the time the weather has been mild and
remarkably pleasant it is true this has been the halcyon dayes,
nature's own repose The vally of the Platt is unique, buitfull,
and healthy beyond description with the exception of some 3 or 4
places where the Bluffs come down to the river, each 6 or 8 miles
over sandy hills, the road is a perfect inclined plane assending
as we pass up the river the banks being but a few feet above the
surface of the river, the bottoms are generaly about ten miles
wide a good soil easely cultivated not so rich as the best land
in Winnebago Co the bluffs and all the land back of the botoms as
far as we have eny knowledge is a sucksession of sand hills with
sufficien grass for sheep pasture if they could have roon enough,
but good for nothing if once ploughed a considerable cotton wood
timber on the banks and numerous isleands. The country on the
North branch is quite different, the bluffs are abbrupt composed
of an earth which I cant describe a mixture of clay and sand softer
than chalk some of it nearly as white in emence solled boddeyes,
and sufficiently tenacious to make the cheapest building material
I ever saw, some specimens might nead a coat of plaster to prevent
the action of the weather but I think not, up to the forks 300 miles
not a stone to throw at a bird nor a rock of aney kind from the
forks 200 miles not a stick to beat a dog with except a very few
scanty willows depended on Buffaloe chips and found them good
enough, in the vicinity of the forks found thousands of Buffaloes
we had the finest fun in the world hunting them I shot a fine young
cow, Oh how I did wish Abby & Charley to see the fun fun it
was sure enough notwithstanding they would sometimes take their

Once our hiking on top of the bluff drew to
a close, we toured the information center and

then toured town in search of an ice cream cone. I yearned for a root beer float, but we both ordered a cherry ice cream cone when I heard the old guy in the old worn-out looking building in the old drive-thru window say, "Well, I don't have roots and I sure don't have beer." He was older than dirt and funny as hell. His ice cream was good and the ice cream "store" was an establishment that has been around since the great flood. It was a perfect place to get small-batch ice cream.

There was much to ponder at day's end and much to study about the exciting next day on this road to discovery. After dinner, we returned to our room for the night and I took up the task of writing down my observations of the day.

LARAMIE, THE PLATTE, AND THE RUTS: JUNE 21

When people take trips, hiccups occur. It's just the way it is. Not knowing the weather, not knowing where to stay, not knowing where to eat are just a few things that can lead to what I like to call travel hiccups.

The latest hiccup occurred today when we checked into our hotel and lugged suitcases, pillows, pills, backpacks, and cooler up to the room. In haste to get an early dinner, we threw things here and there and headed for the eatery. Upon our return, Rayman discovered that the water bottle in his backpack had leaked ... all over the foot of his bed. A discussion ensued. He was hellbent on overheating the hairdryer as he used it on the bed clothes, and I was of the strong opinion that he should call the front desk, fall on his sword, and have housekeeping come up and fix the situation.

This was a hiccup.

However, consider William Henry. His

hiccups could be disastrous. If he didn't tie up or picket his horse, the horse could escape. Picketing is the act of securing the horse to a line so it can graze an area. It prevents the horse from wandering away. Likewise, if he took a wrong turn, he could end up traveling for miles in the wrong direction, only to have to retrace his steps. If he drank bad water, he could perish from cholera. According to the World Health Organization (WHO), "Cholera is an acute diarrhoeal disease that can kill within hours if left untreated." Further, WHO reports, "Severe cases need rapid treatment with intravenous fluids and antibiotics. Provision of safe water and basic sanitation, and hygiene practices is critical to prevent and control the transmission of cholera and other waterborne diseases." In the emigration, most people only knew that it was a disease that killed rapidly.

Such are the differences between 1850 and 2023.

Today we set out to see a series of sights

that were historic and important for William Henry. These sights were important to me too. It promised to be a very interesting journey. We left the town of Scottsbluff and headed north, climbing as we went. Our car took the gradual grade without a problem except for the unsafe speed limits that the state of Wyoming allowed. Nebraska's speed limits were one thing. Wyoming's were beyond the pale. Eighty mph on the freeways. Seventy mph on the two-lane roads with only a painted line between you and the oncoming car or truck. What is the hurry, anyhow? The backroads we traveled were much less busy and we opted for them whenever possible. Most of the trip was on backroads.

Our first stop in Wyoming was at Fort Laramie, where William spent some time on his trip west, as so many other pioneers did. We wandered the grounds of the fort, which was built by the U.S. government. The site was first a trading post. In 1849, the government bought the post in an effort to support the great emigration under way. Seems the politicians were worried about the safety of the emigrants. Fear of the Native Americans drove them to build the fort on the banks of the North Platte River. Strategically it made sense as we gazed across the Platte and tried to imagine the 10,000 Natives who gathered in the area for a meeting to negotiate rules for both parties (the U.S. government and the plains Native Americans) to live by. While that meeting took place after William Henry left to continue his trip west (the treaty was signed September 17, 1851) it still serves as a very, very strong reminder of how important the use of their land was to the plains Natives. The idea was to placate the Native Americans so that they would continue to help the emigrants who were moving west in greater and greater numbers across their territories. This treaty was called the Treaty of Horse Creek. According to the National Park Service (NPS) website the Native participants included, "Oglala Sioux, Assiniboin, Arapaho,

Shoshone (attended though not invited), Brule Sioux, Mandan, Crow, Arikara, Rees, Cheyenne, Gros Ventre, Hidatsa, Snake, The Comanche, Kiowa and Apache refused to attend.

Because the fort could not handle 10,000 American Natives' men, women, and children another spot near the fort was needed. Clearly, the plains Natives wanted to live in peace.

The treaty was broken by the U.S. government and any promise of peace was obliterated. As reported by NPS, "One of the more troublesome aspects of the treaty was the intention of the U. S. Government to hold each tribe responsible for any attacks on American settlers that occurred within their assigned territories. This soon emerged as a major stumbling block in efforts to secure peace.

"The Federal Government promised to protect Indian resources and tribal hunting grounds from depredations by white settlers moving west along the Oregon Trail. This was one of the many promises made in this treaty by the Federal Government that was never kept.

"The U. S. made only one payment, thus breaking the treaty they had fought so hard for. The treaty was redone in 1868 as the *Fort Laramie Treaty of 1868.*"

Nota Bene: William Henry was a man of his time. While educated, his letters were replete with spelling errors, punctuation mistakes, and racial attitudes that are no longer in vogue or appropriate in this day and age. What was written in 1850 (and later) should be taken into consideration of the era, the century in which it occurred. With that in mind, I will share with you his letter about the Native Americans.

Albert & Charles Dresser

My Dear Boyes

     The last letter that I have got from your affectionate Mother
she told me that you were good boyes now that was good news; you
dont know how good it made me feel, I was so glad! now it is two
weeks since I read it and I think of it eny day; Ma could hardly
write enything that would plese me so much as to hear that you are
good boyes. Now little boyes get a little nawghty once in a while,
but if you are very carefull you can be good boyes almost all
the time, Now if you love your Father you will try very hard to be
good—You must be good to your Mother and please her now Pa is
away all you can and be very good to each other, and run and and help
grand Ma & grand Pa do all the little chores for them you can help
Maryett all you can Now when Ma wrote that you good boyes I thought
that I would write you a letter and now I will tel you something
about the Indians that we have seen; the first where the Omahas
pronounced Omahawes oposite Council Bluffs, they are black tall &
slim,rather homely & not very smart, we did not see much of them
we pased through a very little of there country, Then the Panees
pronounced Pawnees they are prity good looking Indians, but the
Sqwas are very smal, quite short, they have to do all the hard work
and carry all the loads, a Frenchman had just been from St Francis,
on the Missoure out to a Panee vilage on the Platt to buy what firs
and Buffaloe skins they had and sold them corn and they where
carying it home, and traveld the same road that we did for we
pased their village, well them great big stout raskals rod on their
Ponies & the Squaws carred about two bushels on their backs and
went afoot we skolded the great lazy fellows but they only laughed
at us, we carried some for them but could not carry much for in
addition to all the rest of our load we then had grain for our
horses. Oh how nasty it dig look to see them eat dead dog, they did
not even skim them just cut them up on the ground sing off the
hair a little and a scortch it on the coles it was sorter burned
& sorter raw but they eat it as though it was mighty good, we
traveled several dayes with them and had a good deal of fun with
them for I find all the Indians like a little fun they talk &
laugh a great deal,—their country extends a long way up the Platt
river— Then we came to the Soux. (Pronounced Soo) they are the
handsomest aborigenes in North America they are very large,
straight beautifull Indians not so black; bright copper collour with
fine open countenance, bigg feeling proud, a large, pourfull
warlike people, all the indians far and near are afraid of them &
hate them they have a great maney horses and mules which in fact
nearly all the tribes have—Then we past through the Crow teritory
but saw none of them neither this nor last years immigration saw

eny of them they live north of the road a good way, the country
runs through the Black Hills up the Sweetwater to the rockey
Mountains,—Then on this side of the Rockey Mountains (what a
thought! Pa on the west side the Rockey Mountains!!) on Green
River head of Rio Colerado of the west & Beer river which are
both in Origon (tel Ma that Pa has been in Origon at last) we
where among the Snake's, a quiet set of chaps, very pleasant and
very good to the immigrants; among them we saw some Flat Heads
& good looking Indians they are,—The next Tribe is the Uta
(Pr Utaw) they are about Salt Lake & Lake Uta they are the
nastyest lazeyest Indians I ever saw, they look mean, dirty,
indolent, shiftless & more than all that they don't know much, they
almost live on crickets of which there are countless Millions,
they are large & different from enything I ever saw the Utaws
live on them in summer and dry them for winter—Then before we
came to the Humbolt all the way down that river (which is some
two hundred miles) up to the Sierra Nevadah mountains & on this
side & a long way north of here are the Shaw Shawnees in English
thier name means root digger for they dig & eat a kind of
artichoke; and on the Humbolt were some that caled themselves
Bious I dont know much about them, but these diggers beat me I
dont know what to make of them, some of them are dreadfull
hostile, thievish, impudent & murderous in the extrieme all the
mischiefe done by the Indians to the emigrants was done by
them, they stole a great maney horses and I am sorry to say
kiled a number of men, Some of them are dreadful ugly looking
and yet meney are prity fair looking, among them on our journey
we found maney that were pleasant. About here are a great maney
of them they dig a good deal of gold and buy considerable
clothing and lots of Beef considerable flour & hard bread there
about every day alwayes peasable, sociable & hardly ever steal,
during the hot wether every once in a while we would see one
among them with nothing but a little rag round their waste with
a little rag for an apron actualy not bigger than my two hands
with nothing behind—, One day one of them came where I was
digging and jabbered a mess of stuf and tuck up my pick (I
suppose he was asking for it) and ran off a little way with it—
well he dug up a hornest nest, struck a match and burned them
with dry [ ] I was ( ) it for one of the yaller jackets
stuck his tale into me a [ ] then he tuck the nest & tied in his
handkerchief to carry home, thinks I what's that for I know they
made no honey for they will get at our fresh beef and eat it
almost as fast as mice so by motiones I asked him if he eat the
grubs that was in the combo & he said [ ] yes & picked them
out and eat them—Now excepting some of these Diggers the indians
helped the emigrants a great deal when cattle & horses would get
frightened & run or stray away the indians would drive them back
sometimes when they had been gone 3 or 4 dayes when they might
just as well of kepet them as not: on Green River our horses got

frightened & some ran 18 miles when I was away some 10 or 12 miles
off alone an indian came to me when I had given up hunting and
toled me by signs where they were and off I went with him 6 or 8
miles further and he went ahead & got & helped drive them in If I
wanted to cross the plains again (which I dont) once clear of the
Diggers, I would not be afraid of the indians to go alone all the
way.
    What have done with the [   ] the Mill stuff did you get
some hoggs?
    Now boyes I wish you would [learn] to spell all you can this
winter; and learn to love God f .[   ] is very good. See how he
[   ] our lives from lightening & all other dangers we should
[   ] God for his loveing kindness everyday—You will find some
choice speamins of Gold one has a small piece of quartz in it—
Tel Ma to write once a month
    Now the best of Heavens blessing rest and abide with Mother
and all you children is the Prayer of your affectionate Father

                               Wm Dresser

Addressed to: Postmark: Culloma   Oct 29
                                    1.20 Alta Cal
    Mrs Sarah Dresser
    Roscoe
    Winnebago Co
    Ill

Back to Fort Laramie for a bit.

The fort became the largest and most well

known fort (on the Northern Plains) in

existence until the 1890s. The era of the Indian

Wars passed. Beavers and other furred animals

were decimated, so the government sold it at a

public auction in 1890. There it sat until 1938

when President Franklin D. Roosevelt's administration added it to the National Park Service's list of historical properties in order to save it from ruin.

The Laramie River and the North Platte converge here so I'm not sure, but when I squatted down to feel the rushing water, I believe it was the water of the Laramie River. I got a big charge out of that because William Henry had been here and may have done the same thing. I also dodged a hiccup. Had I fallen in, I would have been in some trouble. Alas, we left the fort unharmed.

Fun Fact. The visitor's center at the fort has a list of all the pioneers who signed their name on a wall as they passed. In perusing the list, I was disappointed that William's name was not on it. This did not deter our side trip to the cliff, where other pioneers etched their names as they passed through.

That cliff was Register Cliff, our next stop on the road of discovery. What was disheartening was that signatures on the rock included present-day scoundrels. Just as the pioneers obliterated hieroglyphics to make room for their own names on the chalky limestone rock, so did these latter-day travelers. We found it sad. Rayman even saw a signature from someone from Chico, California, dated in the mid-60s. It hurt him because Chico State is his alma mater. He thought people who went there were smarter.

Cow observations. The cows we saw across Nebraska were all huddled together, tails swishing. In Wyoming, the cows wander around and away from one another. We theorized that it was the wind that drove their behavior. We may have been right, we might have been wrong. It was a noticeable difference.

Our final stop for the day was another area the pioneers surely discovered. We veered off the road to visit Ayres Natural Bridge Park. This was where I almost slipped down the mountain. This would not qualify as a hiccup. This would be more like a disaster. There is a difference. But a tree branch saved me as I descended a hill I had no business ascending in the first place. It had loose rocks, uneven rocks, no handrails—it really was a trail for mountain goats. Rayman opted not to climb the rugged trail. Very smart of him.

Ayres Natural Bridge did receive some emigrant visitors. Check it out at en.wikipedia. org/wiki/Ayres_Natural_Bridge_Park

We then resumed our trek and arrived in Casper, Wyoming, our next resting place.

CASPER, WYOMING: JUNE 23

Transitioning from I-80 to Highway 84 was a slight relief. The speed limits decreased to seventy-five. The traffic was much easier to negotiate because there were far fewer trucks. As we zoomed along, I saw a sign: CITY OF ROCKS. I had tried to book a room here but the room was part of a "barracks" with shared baths and the like. No way Rayman was going to approve. So I put CITY OF ROCKS out of my mind—until I saw the sign on the freeway. "Let's go there!" I exclaimed. Rayman was driving and was compliant yet unhappy. Thanking him profusely helped. And away we went. We were happy we did. What a place! It's located in Idaho, but extremely close to Utah and it reminded us of Utah, the land of outstanding national parks.

City of Rocks is not a national park, but a national reserve. No admission fee was required. City of Rocks was recently designated a Dark Sky Preserve, which makes sense because it is out in the middle of nowhere. Wishing I had booked the barracks, we drove into the reserve and what we found was another "register rock." See the pictures below. The emigrants used axle grease to inscribe their names on the rocks (it's hard to carve granite!).

This park is actually part of the California Trail that William was following so it was germane to the task at hand. It was unpaved and dusty until dark clouds arrived and dropped a bit of rain that helped tame the dust. Then lightning arrived and the whole experience was electric. It was worth the detour.

Try to imagine what the pioneers traveling this way must have thought. Many of them were "flatlanders." The plains were relatively flat until the Rockies. Many opted to go over the Rockies via the South Pass, which was known by some to be an easier route for the pioneers, their oxen, horses, and mules. According to Wikipedia, "South Pass, a 20 mile wide, gently sloping gap in the Rocky Mountains, was perhaps the most important landform along the emigrant trails. It opened the West to settlement by providing a route over the Continental Divide that wagons could negotiate" It goes on to report, "Though it approaches a mile and a half high, South Pass is the lowest point on the Continental Divide between the Central and Southern Rocky

Mountains. The passes furnish a natural crossing point of the Rockies. The historic pass became the route for emigrants on the Oregon, California, and Mormon trails to the West during the 19th century. It was designated as a U.S. National Historic Landmark on January 20, 1961."

Of these folks, many came through the City of Rocks before heading toward the Wasatch Mountain passes that led to the Great Salt Lake as well as the South Pass. As a result they really got an eye full of beauty on their trek of a lifetime.

The man at the visitor center, who'd grown up in the area, said the reserve is now enjoying a large number of people because the park has many hiking trails that wind around huge granite boulders, The reserve is 14,000 acres, of which 4,000 allow grazing of cattle.

In 1849 Mr. Bruff, the man sent from Washington, D.C. to chronicle the westward expansion, wrote in his book the following passage:[12]

"August 29, 1849 Frosty early. Patches of snow on the adjacent mountains. We were all white this morning on awakening, with frost, and my hair being very long, the end were froze to the saddle and ground, so that I had to pull it loose, but had to leave some, as a memento for the wolves to examine. We had to look out sharp last night about the Indians."

I thought of the picture in Gulliver's travels, where the Lilliputians had picketed his hair down while he slept. He continued,

"A pack of wolves, this morning, at day-break, saluted us with a reveille. Early breakfast, and soon on the trail again,- which winds up this deep valley, from S.

[12] Bruff, page H1, 116.

by E. round to N.W.—An entire range on our left, of volcanic hills, for about 15 miles: and on our right, similar formations for about 10 ms [miles] when we entered A very extraordinary valley, called the "City of Castles." A couple of miles long, and probably 1/2 mile broad, A light grey decrepitating granite, (probably altered by fire) in blocks of every size, from that of a barrel to the dimensions of a large dwelling-house; groups, Masses on Masses and Cliffs; and worn, by the action of ages of elementary affluences, into strange and romantic forms. The travellers had marked several large blocks as their fancy dictated the resemblance to houses, castles,, &c.—On one was marked (with tar) 'NAPOLEON'S CASTLE,' another,

'CITY HOTEL,' &c. We nooned [had lunch] among these curious monuments of nature. I dined hastily, on bread and water, and while others rested, I explored and sketched some of these queer rocks. A group, on the left of the trail, resembled gigantic fungii, petrified, other clusters were worn in cells and caverns; and one, which contrasted with the size and height of the adjacent rocks, seemed no larger than a big chest, was, to my astonishment, when close it, quite large, hollow, with an arch'd entrance, and capable of containing a dozen persons."

Bruff's book contained sketches of the rocks we took pictures of here. Again, it is so interesting to have stood on the ground of Mr. Bruff and all others that transited this way, including William Henry. It was an honor to be there.

This passage tells us many things about the area in 1849. It was cold in the mornings in late August. There was scant food to eat many days. Wolves were all around. It illustrates how scurvy was problematic for the emigrants in general. It also illustrates how the emigrants kept up communication with each other as they passed various landmarks.

For additional information, check en.wikipedia.org/wiki/City_of_Rocks_National_Reserve

Scurvy is disease that presents itself when of lack of vitamin C occurs. Eating citrus fruits helps to avoid that disease. Nowadays, we have vitamin C in tablet form so scurvy is much less common that it had been in the past.

Regarding animals, we have not seen a skunk. We saw a dead snake in the road that looked to be about six feet long. Deer, dead deer, have been the most frequent roadkill. A few badgers, and a fox are about all the wild animals we've seen. This has been a bit disappointing. No, it has been terribly

disappointing because we have not seen a
buffalo, a bison. Bison in the millions roamed
the grasslands of the plains in the 1800s. No
more. Very sad. And we have not seen any
antelope playing.

For an excellent documentary, watch Ken
Burns's two-part series on the buffalo on PBS.

Like the bison, the wolf was nearly wiped
out by the 1950s as farmers killed all they
could because the wolves were known to
attack stock animals. Sportsmen also hunted
wolves for sport. This was all sanctioned by
the government.

Today, I'm happy to report that bison herds
are making a comeback as are wolves. PBS
reports, "It was not until the late sixties, when
a greater understanding of natural ecosystems
began changing attitudes in the scientific
community and the National Park Service,
that the plight of wolves in North America
began to improve."

Regarding bison recovery, I found this on
the American Prairie website, "Although some

progress has been made, the bison's recovery has been slow and is far from complete. Hundreds of thousands of bison remain in North America today, with most being raised for commercial uses in herds on small acreages behind fences. Less than ten percent of existing bison are managed for conservation or as a wild species. Thousands of bison on large landscapes are needed to fulfill their former ecological role. Moreover, most conservation herds are very small, numbering in the dozens to a few hundred, and are mostly confined to small, fenced-in areas. These conditions threaten the genetic health of bison and greatly hinder their ability to roam widely and display natural behaviors. This combination of genetic, ecological, and behavioral concerns makes bison restoration a high priority for wildlife conservation in North America. Keep up to date with bison conservation and recovery at: IUCN Red List." You can find more info at their website, americanprairie. org/bison-restoration.

Back to William Henry. He successfully reached California before the snow in Sierras. This was the plan. With the fate of the Donner Party etched in their brains, I'm sure every person making the trip after 1847 planned their trip to avoid such a calamity. That calamity being a party of emigrants who perished near Donner Lake because of incessant snow storms that prevented them from reaching shelter. As it turned out in 1850, precipitation started in November according to the Sierra Sun newspaper, so William easily made it to his destination before the first snow that year.

To put a finer point on it, according to Britannica, "The Sierra Nevada is an asymmetrical range with its crest and high peaks decidedly toward the east. The peaks range from 11,000 to 14,000 feet (3,350 to 4,270 metres) above sea level, with Mount Whitney, at 14,494 feet (4,418 metres), the highest peak in the coterminous United States. Summits in the northern portion are much lower, those north of Lake Tahoe reaching altitudes of only 7,000 to 9,000 feet." To gaze up at the Sierra Nevada range from the east, is to behold beauty beyond ones' imagination. It is breath-taking. I highly recommend a trip on highway 395 from Mojave to the Oregon border to see for yourself. Or the other way around.

Another quote from Mr. Bruff shows the travails that women endured while traveling during the Gold Rush. In July 1850 Mr. Bruff was in the area of Lassen, California which was northwest of the gold fields of Sutter's Mill. He arrived in California using the Lassen cut-off aka as the Emigrant's cut-off after taking a vote of his company. They believed it was a faster way to get where they were going. It did not involve gold. Remember, his company was collecting data. One of his more memorable passages in his book describes an amazing event:

"On the ride out, at the deep hollow—some 20 miles from the

settlements, the Frenchman's squaw, had to dismount, and cause a slight detention, while she gave birth to a child; It was enveloped in a rag and its mother mounted her poney astraddle, in half an hour, after, with the infant mountaineer, and rode about 35 miles, without any serious inconvenience. The child did not survive the ride and was buried."[13]

This passage illustrates the toughness of the people of the day. No further explanation is needed. And you can bet this happened with some frequency along the trail west. Graves of children are mentioned throughout his book. But in this case, we witness the mother coping with what is dealt to her in a nearly unimaginable way.

Again, this illustrates how rough and tumble

---

[13] Bruff, pages 372-373

it was for women in the West. While Miss Kitty was glamorized as the owner of the saloon, far more women had a completely different experience. Between childbirth and cooking for the miners, they led a hard life too. If they made it all the way to California, they discovered a wild time around the mining camps. Outdoor plumbing was a necessity until a cabin could be built. Then it was often outdoor plumbing still.

It really took me reading Bruff's book to realize something I didn't think about before: that the entire trip involved camping. There were no Hampton Inns. There were no restaurants. Many women decided they needed to make bread (money) because their husbands were not finding gold. The men toiled in the streams and the mines without guarantee that gold or silver or other metals would be found. Women took up the slack. They baked bread. They roasted meat. They concocted soup out of whatever was available. And they sold or bartered food to keep the family afloat. The women also ran boarding houses and provided meals to renters. Their work was hard but they often out-earned their husbands who'd spent the day panning for gold. Some women thrived and became rich from their hard work.

Food was elemental. Deer, oxen, mules, ravens, squirrels, ducks, geese, horses, bears, fish, wolves, rats, even. It was eat or be eaten. Bread was the mainstay. Hard bread and coffee was often the only thing available if animals or fish were unavailable.

As time went along, the situation changed but in 1850, this is how it was. This is what William Henry experienced, no doubt.

June 24

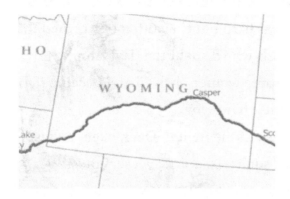

Getting a late start was not in our plan, yet we managed to start late. Plans were important and we realized we needed to do better.

We left Casper, Wyoming, this morning and headed north, south, and west. Backroads led us in different directions but the routes were usually really good if we were not in a hurry. Today was a good day on the backroads. The best stop of the day was at Independence Rock, a granite boulder that reminded us of a smaller version of Ayers Rock ("Uluru" is the new Indigenous name) in the Outback of Australia. It wasn't the biggest thing around, but it was impressive to the pioneers and to us. We did not climb it as many trail travelers do.

When the emigrants visited the rock, they did climb it. From Mr. Bruff's note,

"July 26, Commences with fly(g) clouds, light breeze from the N.E. Temp. 62. Company seem in good spirits. Independence Rock at a distance looks like a huge whale. It is painted and marked every way, all over, with names, dates, initials, &c - so that it was great difficulty I could find a place to inscribe on it: - "The Washington City Comp(y) July 26, 1849."[14]

At this point, we wished we were a bit younger so we could scale the rock. This is in addition to all the other times we wish we were a bit younger!

Heading past the rock, we traversed a high plateau of about 5,500 feet elevation on average. We would go up, we would go down, and every time we looked at the app, it seemed

---

[14] Bruff, Vol, 1, page 22.

we were around 5,500 feet.

Today there were hiccups that can be explained away as, "We were tired and cranky, and mad at our phones." First of all, Casper was cold and cranky. As we headed here and there, the wind was playful, then serious. The mountains were red and then they were brown, then they were green. A beautiful ride until we hit a storm that rose up from seemingly nowhere. The sky darkened to charcoal black, the freeway was under construction for mile upon mile and straddling a roughed-up area in the only lane going our way was the order of the day. We were jousted around by new ruts, potholes. When the storm got going, lightning struck and rain pelted us with raindrops the size of tennis balls. While we slowed down, huge trucks rumbled by and sprayed us with road rain mist so that we had to slow down to fifty mph so I could see the highway to drive. The speed limit was seventy-five and people here in their big F-150s and huge trucks did not slow down. It was frightening. But we were dry in our Rogue.

Today, we viewed the Wasatch Mountains from the north. The mountain range was high and snow-capped and looked formidable. I wonder what the view was like for William Henry as he approached Salt Lake City. I also marveled about how high and generally flat the route through the South Pass was for the pioneers. My idea of the Rockies was that they were rugged with deep gorges. This is not at all what the South Pass land is like today. The ups and downs were mostly gradual with grassy hillsides. This was a revelation. The pioneers had paid good attention to the fur trappers' routes and Native Americans' routes and had chosen wisely.

One hiccup was turning the wrong way for a nice ten-mile detour, our second so far on this trip. Third hiccup was that Rayman booked dinner in Evanston, Illinois, instead of Evanston, WYOMING. Fourth hiccup was that I double-booked our room. I booked a room on-line earlier in the trip, and I booked a room on the phone on the way into town. I hoped we would get our money back. So, while William Henry knew his route, he may not have gotten lost. And he couldn't book dinner because there were no restaurants, no phones. Could it be said that life was harder, yet less complicated? I wonder about these things.

It was an amazing trip because the views were spectacular. The cliffs changed colors, funny-shaped rocks shot up to the sky, rivers and streams rolled along, turning here, turning there. The amount of times the road crossed the Platte River was surprising but uneventful and not unexpected based on my research. When the pioneers crossed the Platte each time, it was a major accomplishment. Wheels would break, wheels would get stuck in the river bottom. Covered wagons would flip over. People would drown.

Now, there are bridges for safe passage. There are rest stops. We are blessed.

A word about present-day Wyoming. We

did not enjoy the unsafe speeds on any of the highways. We never knew for sure where we were because of sparse signage. Want to know how far it is to XYZ? We needed a GPS. There was nary a sign to announce anything important, like the name of the next town and the mileage to it. Our GPS malfunctioned a lot in Wyoming. We were wondering if we were being subjected to interference from outer space (Starlink?).

Of course, back in 1850 there were no highways. We needed to remind ourselves how fortunate we had been this entire journey. Blending paper and digital magic helped us time and again.

Tonight we are roosting in a Best Western motel, with a restaurant attached. We walked down to the joint and ordered a martini, and split a glass of red wine with dinner. Four big, young guys sat at the table in front of our booth. The T-shirts they wore indicated they were gun guys. As we left, I could not help myself. I sauntered up to their table as Rayman attempted to blend into the wallpaper on the wall. The guys were long-range sharpshooters and were in town for a competition. So, I asked where they lived. One lived in Santa Cruz, California, another in San Diego, California. The third guy lived in Atascadero, California. and when he announced this, I felt compelled to reveal that I was born in Atascadero (remember the mud hole?). We all got a kick out of the conversation. Which just shows you, doesn't it? The world is very small sometimes, even when it seems so enormous.

This hotel was my favorite of the trip. It was a motel: all one story with parking spots in front of the windows of each room. The vibe was mid-last century and comfy. A Best Western at its finest.

The next morning, we perused the "free breakfast" and took a pass. We were not double charged for our room because the place was packed. And so we left Evanston, Wyoming, to turn north toward Boise, Idaho, once we found out where we were... because we got lost getting out of town.

From what I deduce from his written record, William Henry arrived in Salt Lake City mid-June, 1850.

City of the Great Salt Lake   June 19/50

My Dear Sarah

By the Goodness of an All Wise and Gracious Providence I am
able to write to you again the wayes of God has been very
fabourable to me thus far My health is good and has been thus
far. We have made rapid progress   counting those on both side of
the Platt we have pased some two thousand teams the grass has
not been eaten ahead of us, none has pased us, we arrived here
yesterday, and I have divided with Otis, have got plenty of
provisions and I took one horse which I swaped for a 6 year old
mare wintered in the Mountains a full sized American and
perfectly fresh in this I have made will provision is very
scarce here some will be obleged to wait til harvest some 3 weeks
I shall of course walk considerable until my load gets lighter.
I shall try to get it carried more or les. I owe Otis $18 to
put in the Mines. Mare is a an able boded active one she was
tied up all night this morning have got her shod so she is tied
up yet I must write fast, as far as the roads mountains rivers
hardships are conserned the jouiney is past time. But Oh my
Heavens how men quarrill   I am ashamed to be a man   Otis & I
disagreed so we disolved the Division will amount to my
advantage very much only if I cant get my provisions carried I
shall walk so much more it will take from 25 to 30 dayes yet I
hope that you all have been blessed with health as will a myself
I also hope not be disapointed in hearing from you and my
Children so soon as I arrive at the mines an continialy at least
once a month, the other Beloit Co that left so long before us
took the Fort Hall road. Day before we got to the forks they where
dreadfuly out with Hilier—the next 600 miles is over a good
road then 150 over the Nevady Mountains very bad, my hungry
horse excuses me from writing more in detail   I have now $6,00
cash some things more to dispose that I cant well cary plenty of
clothing vintcuals (best cind) a fresh horse sadle & bridle and
thank God good health and Spirits

Humbly trusting in that same
Providence
I am Yours in Gods Love
Wm Dresser

Addressed to: Postmark: none
    Mrs Sarah Dresser
    Roscoe   Postage: 10¢
    Winnebago Co
    Ill

Page 21

Return Address
    Mr William Dresser
    Sacramento Cit
    Calafornia

We got back to Highway 84 and zoomed up to Boise, Idaho to visit relatives who had recently relocated to the outskirts of the city. We decided to return to the Pacific Northwest rather than continue the trip west because we had crossed the Great Basin years before. In retrospect, that was a silly idea. So, as often happens, we changed our mind and decided to pick up the trail again in Elko, Nevada, and follow it to Coloma, California. This decision was made as we reflected on how much fun the trip had been and how important it was to finish it off right.

To continue our travels, we took a right to head north back to Portland, but William Henry continued to head for the Sierra Nevada Mountains in the summer of 1850. He planned to mostly walk. The map of the California Trail available through the National Park Service website shows that there were several paths to the Sierras from Salt Lake City that most emigrants used. Through my extensive research, I believe he took the northern route.

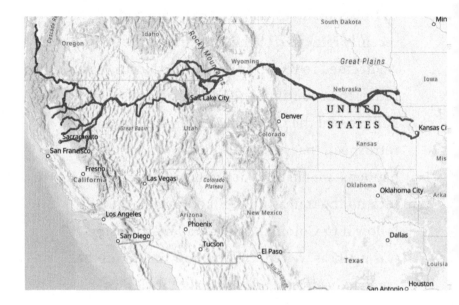

Whether that is fact or not is up for debate. However, the map also shows that those two paths meet up near Elko before heading further west so I think it fair to assume he ventured through Elko.

Have you ever been to Elko, Nevada? Allow me to share my experience. We have been to Elko. In December1990, Rayman and I stayed all night in Elko. It was thirty-three below zero. It gets cold in Elko. So cold that our car

innards froze up and we could not start our
Plymouth Voyager in order to continue our
trip to Salt Lake City to ski. The other thing to
know is one should never wear Levi's in that
kind of cold. This was a learned experience. Of
course, unbeknownst to me, my great-great-
grandfather had been to Elko but it was
summertime. Elko temperature data starts in
1890 so what he suffered through temperature-
wise is unknown.

My money is on hot.

As we merged onto one of the only big
freeways of this entire trip, our GPS went on
the fritz.

However, back in the Gold Rush days, life
was a million times harder, as this writer
notes: "A wagon capsized, the stock
stampeded, an overcharged gun exploded, a
man run over by a wagon, a death from
cholera, a hunter unhorsed in a buffalo
hunt—such were the common incidents of the

California Trail."[15]

This illustrates what my great-great grandmother Sarah feared—and she was right to do so as she had physical ailments and was often sick in bed. Even with her weak constitution, she managed childbirth. Childbirth was not risk free and it is not risk free even today. In her time, many mothers died, or their babies died during childbirth. She was wise to remain in Winnebago/Beloit/ Roscoe area.

So off we charged from Evanston, Wyoming, on I-80 where the speed limit was eighty and there were miles and miles and miles of road construction. Every road we have taken on this trip has been under repair or expansion. Build Back Better (a new government program) is working. Maybe it's a pain in our derrières, those who are braving the roads, but this work is boosting the economy and improving our infrastructure

---

[15] Bruff, Page xlix

just as the pioneers did in 1850–1860.

Back then new trails were forged, old trails forgotten. After people reached California, many worked on trail improvements from the west to the east. But not everyone stayed once they arrived in California and Oregon. Some stopped mid-trip and turned tail back to where they came from. Many made it and decided they missed their friends, families, and the comforts of the home they left. So in that regard, some things never change... change is always happening (and this includes the work on trails and roads).

FROM ELKO TO THE MINES OF CALIFORNIA

Before we take off to complete this journey by traveling from Portland, Oregon, to Elko, Nevada, and on into California via the Carson Trail, I have spent time on the computer looking at our planned route. This activity furthered my involvement with the Oregon-California Trail Association. Let me introduce the organization to you.

Anyone can join the group. It was formed to provide an organization of people keen on preserving the trails the emigrants traveled. The work they do is invaluable. They find and mark the wagon wheel ruts across the country.

An example. They have a website. They have a YouTube channel. They are modern users of social media. Through them I found great books about the Gold Rush, great maps to follow. As a matter of fact, Bob Black, a long-time member, has written many guides, including the one we will use for the last part of our journey, *The California Trail Along the*

Humboldt River (fifth edition).

A GUIDE TO
THE CALIFORNIA TRAIL
ALONG THE HUMBOLDT RIVER
Fifth Edition

BOB BLACK

AN EMIGRANT TRAILS WEST SERIES GUIDEBOOK
BY
TRAILS WEST, INC., RENO, NEVADA

If I had been smarter and quicker, I would

have discovered all the various Trails West books years ago. See emigranttrailswest.org. What this group has done is quite remarkable and I highly recommend a visit if you are interested in the history (or seeing the ruts).

But, hey, better late than never. Wait. Maybe I should make the trip again with all their guides! Rayman would need coaxing. In that vein, I found this program on YouTube and we watched it. It's where we learned about an organization called Mountain Men. Quite impressive. And preserving Gravelly Ford. It is near Elko, so we plan a visit.

youtu.be/PSaVs859Zqg

Just enter the above address into your browser to watch this presentation.

Now it is time to complete the journey that William Henry Dresser made by getting back to the trail he took from Elko to California.

Dateline: Oct. 24, 2023

We left Portland this morning to travel east, then south. Having never ventured into much of the eastern part of the state, we were delighted to find John Day, Oregon.

John Day is the town near the John Day River. It's a five-hour drive through a magnificent landscape of national forests, looming mountains, gurgling creeks, meandering rivers. We were blown away, but not by the rain that christened us as we blasted east on Highway 84 through the Columbia Gorge. A trip worth taking. Lady Luck must have played a part in leading us this way.

As I said, taking this route was part of our effort to get to Elko, Nevada, to finish the trip of discovery. We were blessed by the travel gods. Yes, rain was an impediment, but not much of one because as we moved east, the rain lessened. Yes, windshield wipers were engaged, but once we left Highway 84, we had the road south to ourselves. We passed maybe ten cars in eighty miles. There were many more head of cattle than cars. Perfect.

Arriving in John Day, we checked into our hotel, a two-story affair where we scored a downstairs room. Downstairs rooms are good because we bring everything but the proverbial kitchen sink, plus Beau, our adorable labradoodle. All the luggage must be loaded and unloaded for each stay. And the place has no elevator, so downstairs is a blessing for this family.

After unloading the car, we found a good bar and grill within walking distance. History and historical context was on the menu mid-day. By dinner time, food took center stage and the wine helped us to relax and enjoy the dinner. We had a great time.

Since William Henry traveled south of here, I have nothing to report on this front. As a reminder, he headed south out of the City of Rocks to Salt Lake City.

Oct. 25, 2023

Up at 8:00 a.m. and rain falling. Not hard, but it was cold. The tops of the mountains near the town of John Day were covered with a blanket of snow. Very pretty and first of the season.

In the car, we retraced yesterday's steps back on Highway 19. As we traveled, the sun popped through. We saw the scenery but it was completely different now because of the sunshine. The mountains were radiant, giving us an "eye-candy" experience! The valley was green and dotted with black cows. The layers of rock turned colors, granting us a glimpse of the area's geological history. Whisking ourselves down to the Thomas Condon Interpretive Center, we stopped to view the displays and ask questions.

Fossils discovered here have been shipped all over the world for educational purposes. This 14,000-square-mile area is famous for fossils. At one time (44 million years ago), this place was a verdant tropical forest and home to elephants, camels, hippos—to name a few surprising inhabitants. Through the ages, volcanos erupted and spewed ash and lava that killed the habitat. Then it rained. Then new flora grew, new animals adapted just like Charles Darwin surmised, and then the volcanos erupted and started the cycle all over again. Thus, when you view the mountains here, you can travel through geological time. Fascinating. Oregon is a great state to put on the bucket list for volcano fans.

The emigrants, may have seen some volcanic activity. According to the state website, "Between 1843 and 1860, a series of 21 eruptions took place in the Cascades."[16] These eruptions would not affected William Henry, but those emigrants traveling to Oregon to farm in the area may have experienced nature making itself know.

Thomas Cordon was the real fossil sleuth. He was Oregon's first state geologist.

---

[16] oregon.gov/dogami/volcano/pages/volcanoes.aspx

Originally a minister from the East who had been very interested in geology from an early age, he was a man of some renown in geology circles. I have an idea: Thomas Cordon should replace John Day (a trapper with no geological training). The current naming is akin to having a Yogi Berra Stadium in Arizona.

So, quite a time viewing fossils, taking a short hike, and enjoying the Wild West that William Henry never saw.

Oct. 26, 2023

Today was another long day on the road, but it was different this time. Heading out of John Day (the town), we climbed a series of summits as we reached for the sky. Snow was everywhere and there was ice on the road. Beautiful but nerve racking since we can't put chains on the tires of our all-wheel drive vehicle. Rayman masterfully drove through the forests on the almost-deserted highway. Miles and miles with no other car in sight. Backroads are just the best... unless you want a cup of coffee. It took us about four hours to find coffee. While caffeine was hard to find, cows were not. Everywhere we went, there were cows. Cows in the valleys, cows on the hills, cows behind trees, cows on the road. We had it all. Except coffee.

The mountains looked blue, then brown. Clouds were puffy and white, puffy and dark gray, but they withheld their rain so we could traverse the land without windshield wipers. A plus.

And the backroads are well paved and well marked. That was true in Oregon, and it was true in Idaho, our destination. Twin Falls, Idaho. The roads were a pleasure to drive.

The desk clerk at our hotel gave us some bad news. Twin Falls weren't falling. Invasive mussels had invaded the Snake, so they "turned the river off." "Only a trickle now," our tattooed desk clerk said. Good grief. They obviously didn't know WE were coming.

The highlight of the trip was a four-mile detour to look at Boise Valley from on high. The Oregon-California Trail Association (OCTA) erected a viewing spot that looked down at the region (including wagon ruts!). Below is a photo. It's called the Bonneville Point. Great view—and ruts.

It was getting colder and colder. Lucky for us to be tucked in bed for a warm, restful sleep! Only it was not restful. Someone above us was thumping around. Rayman fell dead asleep but I suffered two hours with nary a wink. Called the front desk twice to no avail. Finally passed out from exhaustion, I presume. My overactive mind conjured a vision of Simone Biles practicing gymnastics above our heads.

When it was cold at the higher elevations in 1850, William Henry had to endure much more than we did. He never wrote about this so I will again turn to J. Goldsborough Bruff for his experience at the time.

"I sat up late to night, writing notes and plotting down memorandums for several day's march ahead: At last, having completed my memorandums, by the light of the flickering camp-fire, and chilled with the cool air, I button'd my over coat close about me, rolled up in a blanket, with my head on an old saddle for a pillow, and went off, also, to the land of Nod."[17]

From this account, we learn that night-time fires were built when it was cold, the emigrants slept in their clothes, and they tried to keep warm with blankets. But, William Henry never spoke these survival issues. Perhaps he did not want to worry Sarah.

If it rained, many emigrants had brought

---

[17] Bruff, page 63.

with them 'Indian Rubber coats," first
patented in the early 1820s by a man in
Scotland. It provided some protection from
rain and snow. Today the market is flooded
with all types of garments for protection from
the elements. Think North Face, Patagonia.
Think fleece and other new materials.

What gets me are the shoes. The emigrants
had leather boots as rubber boots did not
appear until 1853, the year William Henry
returned to his family in Beloit. If leather
boots got wet, that spelled trouble. Bruff once
fell in some water when the temperature was
low.

"Reached nearly the Summit about 11 p.m.
very cold,—but there was plenty of fine dry
willow logs, pieces of a broken wagon, and any
quantity of dead brush, on our left, in the
woods. So we soon had a rousing fire, in the
middle of the road.—Smoked our pipes, drew
straws for guard, spread our blankets on the
sloping bank on left, feet to the fire, and heads
against the trees, the sentinel sat on the end of

a large log near the fire, and the others threw themselves, with saddles under their heads, on their pallets & were soon snoring."[18]

In another account, one of Bruff's men traded his boots for moccasins. The Native Americans were on to something, perhaps. In the East, soles of the native footwear were soft for walking through forests with an understory of fallen leaves: but in the West, the soles of moccasins were hard in order to handle the rocks, sagebrush, and the like. Overall, trading boots for moccasins was not an uncommon trade.

And finally, as Bruff reports, "I was tired, the night cold, and I had no bedding but a thin horse-blanket, but a couple of clever lads, of the company... pressed me to share their bed, which I accepted, and we dozed off the cold night very well." This was not a one-off. Many books on the Gold Rush mention this practice of sharing body heat in passing.

---

[18] Bruff, page 97

All in all, another great day cruising the countryside while considering the differences that happen over time.

Oct. 27, 2023

Twin Falls is a very new-looking town. All the regular suspects at the strip malls. Walmart looms. I got a "twofer" deal on gloves at Dick's Sporting Goods. A sale was underway, just in time to save my fingers from the risk of morning frostbite. The forecast for Elko, Nevada (today's destination): very cold.

While William Henry could have traded for gloves, he could not have popped into a Dick's Sporting Goods. As the emigration continued over the decade, trading posts with new inventory came into being along the overland trails. Maybe he could have purchased gloves in one of those establishments.

So off we went on Highway 93 south to explore the Great Basin. Thanks to Ryan, our son, we learned earlier that the Great Basin has no water that flows out of it to the ocean. Hence the name. Today we found the genesis of the Humboldt River, which springs forth from terra firma. Our intention is to follow it to the Humboldt Sink near Carson City,

Nevada. A sink is where a river terminates into the earth. There the river disappears. Our intention is to also see the ruts from the wagons that traversed the landscape back in the 1800s.

Two great discoveries today. First, we saw some ruts outside of Wells, Nevada. Wells is a spot in the road. Train tracks run through it. Of course, in 1850 there were no train tracks. And there were no run-down buildings like there are today. And there was no Interstate 80. Between the train tracks and interstate, many of the ruts have been obliterated, unfortunately for rut seekers like us.

We drove on a dirt road to the marker for the California trail.

And then we drove to the Interpretive Center west of Elko (about ten miles off I-80). Great place! If you're ever near the area, a stop is well worth your time. Lots of history is presented about the pioneers' trek west. The center is a collaborative effort between OCTA and the Bureau of Land Management (BLM) and the Department of the Interior. We are fortunate to have a government that spends time and money to support history.

While humming along in our car, we discussed the hardships these brave men and women and their children endured. The sagebrush was everywhere. The sand and silt rendered the journey an almost impossible trip. Imagine sand in all your belongings. Image sifting sands so thick the livestock often died from its effects. And then multiply that by all the days across the basin, thirty to forty days of hell on earth. And yet they persisted. By a variety of accounts, this basin was dreaded because on top of the sand and sagebrush was the crushing desert heat.

According to the Nevada State Historic Preservation organization, "A count made in 1850 showed these appalling statistics for Forty Mile Desert: 1,061 dead mules, about 5,000 dead horses, 3,750 dead cattle and oxen, and 953 emigrant graves."

After a two-hour visit, we returned to Elko. Had a great Mediterranean meal of lamb chops, hummus, and tabouleh washed down with some zinfandel in an unassuming restaurant. The moon was full. Back at our hotel, I found no good TV channels (imagine that!) so was left to pound away on my computer to record our history of the day. It is all history, isn't it?

The elevation is 5,630 feet here, and the wine is working. Yippie!

Oct. 28, 2023

Lollygagged in the morning because frost was covering everything outside. Better to let it melt. It was the first frost warning of the impending winter. After things warmed up, we jumped in the car and headed out to buy pasties for breakfast. No, I did not misspell it. Pasties, while originating in Europe, are now an Elko, Nevada thing and described as food for the miners who used to prospect in the surrounding hills of Nevada as they searched for silver. I was reminded that many cultures devised hand-held food that was easy to eat while working...pasties provided that for the miners. This is a good reminder that while gold caused a rush, silver and other precious metals were also mined by the emigrants. Sweet pasties are basically small pies. Mine was rhubarb and Rayman's was blueberry. Then we went to Bob's Coffee and ordered the "special." It was basically a latte made with condensed milk. Boy, was it good. Way to go, Bob!

Filled the tank and headed out on I-80, where you can drive eighty miles an hour. Traffic was scant for a major interstate. The trucks must use other routes because they were few and far between. We covered lots of land quickly. After leaving Wyoming we thought eighty mpg was not going to be experienced again in our future travels. Wrong.

A word about the land. Oh, those poor emigrants! In order to reach northern California, they had to endure travel through the Great Basin. While they struggled across on existing trails that followed the Humboldt, the entire basin covers 200,000 square miles. What a fright that must have been for them because after 1849, most knew the high desert of the Great Basin must be crossed to reach the Sierra Nevada mountain range. And then there were the Sierras to cross into California.

According to the National Park Service website, "The Great Basin Desert is defined by plant and animal communities. The climate is affected by the rain shadow of the Sierra

Nevada and Cascade Mountains. It is a
temperate desert with hot, dry summers and
snowy winters. The valleys are dominated by
sagebrush and shadescale. The biologic
communities on the mountain ranges differ
with elevation, and the individual ranges act as
islands isolated by seas of desert vegetation.
Because the Great Basin exhibits such drastic
elevation changes from its valleys to its peaks,
the region supports an impressive diversity of
species, from those adapted to the desert to
those adapted to forest and alpine
environments."

As the pioneers trudged west, their progress
was intercepted by one mountain range after
another. Mostly they followed the Humboldt
River for survival so climbing up and down
mountains did not occur often. The Humboldt
River originates near the town of Wells,
Nevada at a location known as Humboldt
Wells. Presently that local is privately owned.
The Humboldt was a miserable river because it
meandered all over the basin, thereby

guaranteeing the emigrants had to weave back and forth rather than travel straight as they followed it until it terminated at the Humboldt Sink. As mentioned earlier, a "sink" is where a river disappears into marshes and returns to the earth. The Humboldt Sink is located near Carson City, Nevada.

Pioneers had a love-hate relationship with the river. It was wide in parts but very shallow. It yielded little except willow branches, disagreeable mosquitoes, putrid water, and some grasses that the livestock could eat, according to Bruff as well as other authors and diarists. By the time the pioneers reached the Great Basin, they were already in dire straits. The oxen were skin and bones, the mules not much better. Horses probably fared the best because they could be ridden to grass and water. It was hell on earth for the emigrants.

By the time they reached the Great Basin near Elko, Nevada, they had abandoned almost everything they had brought. This last part of the journey was often done on foot because wagons had been left on the trail, used as firewood, or overturned in a river and abandoned. Therefore, only the critical provisions were carried by the mules and oxen. Oxen were not well designed for this. Their body shape did not accommodate luggage. They were more sure-footed than mules and horses but items kept falling off their backs because their skin drooped. As they withered away, they were often shot and butchered and eaten by the travelers. Mules fared better, but they were not as strong (except in their attitudes).

William Henry writes of his experience after reaching the California gold fields. His letter[19] was written at "Kellsey's Diggins near Coloma, Eldorado Co California, Oct 13, 1850.

"With respect to my Exodus across the wilderness (falsely called Plains for

19 I transcribed this letter as written with misspellings and punctuation issues.

that term is only applicable to the valley of the Platt) I got a head of every one I started with except Fargo who killed two or three horses got starved out & got in a head of all—Carter and the rest of Cap Hick's train came into or three days after me Otis about a week later: Br. Pennman of all those we left at the Bluffs arrived first and alone I think near the middle of Agst the rest of our Beloit train strung along at intervals until late in Sept. I have not heard from all, I fear from what I have that one of the Bennetrs Died in Carson valley at the east foot of the Nevada- otherwise all of our trains and those from Roscoe (I have not heard from enemy of the Roscoe immigrants for several weeks) as far as known are all alive and in good health, the sickle season is now past-I out traveled Hicks for we I e Fargo, Otis and myself went by Salt Lake some 3 or 4 days out of our way and then fell in with him at the head of the Humbolt and I gained on the Badger train so that almost trod on the boys heels I had no affliction no distress yet the journey was waring and tedious for I had not a single hours leisure for 72 days, each morning up at 3 and about 10 to bed at night, since my arrival I have gained flesh and fatter now than you ever saw me my weight is about 158—Some of those from Beloit who arrived late suffered horribly Banty never expected to get through and he was so ugly that no one would have cared if he had not"

So, back to present day. How was our trip across the Great Basin, other than fast? We did not have to bothered with the alkaline soil. No dust. No mosquitoes. Oh yeah, and we were *in a car*. It was a lovely drive and we talked about how much the emigrants suffered as they traveled about twenty-five miles a day. We did not have much wind today. They encountered terrific winds which blew the sand and silt. Our road was very straight. Their road was meandering; the trail followed the schizophrenic river as it twisted and turned throughout its route (as noted earlier). The pioneers had to follow it to stay alive. Water was precious—even if putrid. Incidentally, the word "pioneer" generally refers to the first who is among those who first enter or settle a region, thus opening it for occupation and development by others, according to several dictionaries I searched.

Livestock drowned in the river. The emigrants drank the river water anyway. I read an account somewhere that they would take a blanket, capture some water, squeeze that water through the blanket to "clean" it, then let it drip into a bowl Then they filled their water carriers, usually a canteen, with this water so they could drink as they traveled. Lord knows how many died from drinking that contaminated water. As cholera is generally associated with drinking bad water, this process probably led many emigrants to their graves. Cholera was and is a virulent disease that caused runny diarrhea and lead to death if untreated. Dehydration was caused by cholera and with water being scarce, dehydration was quite prevalent.

Mirages were also a problem for the overlanders. Parched and dying of thirst, they would spot a mirage in the forty miles of desert that abuts the Sierras. People and livestock stampeded to the mirage, only to find alkaline soil glittering in the sun. What a cruel hoax!

In another book authored.by Joseph Henry Jackson, *The Gold Rush Album*. Mr. Jackson writes, "The Wells of the Humboldt, sometimes gave rise to a strange and unsatisfactory river, none to full, none too sweet, hemmed in by high and barren mountains from whose flanks rose slender smoke columns to show that the thieving Digger Indians were watching for a chance to raid and steal the animals that stood between you and death in a desert. The trail ran sometimes along the banks with good grass, then sometimes high up on naked spurs. There were no trees. The sun beat down, the dust was blown in your face by constant west wind; always the dust in your food, in your drink, chafing your skin. It was best to travel by night when others were asleep and the restless wheels ahead were not churning up the trail. There were almost three hundred miles of it; from the source of the Humboldt to Lassen's Meadows."[20]

Interstate 80 had been repaved so Rayman and I had an enjoyable ride. We took it at seventy-five mph. It's sobering to realize that

---

[20] Jackson, Joseph Henry, Charles Scribner's Sons, (New York), 1949.

our one hour of driving equaled *three days' travel* for the emigrants. We felt pangs of guilt for having such a trouble-free trip.

Dateline: Oct. 29, 2023

The last leg of our journey. What a day it was! We headed into the Sierra Nevada mountains on the route known as Ebbetts Pass. Every twist and turn led us to yet another eye-candy scene. The Ebbetts Pass website reports the following:

> "Glacially carved valleys, granite outcroppings, basalt columns, ancient volcanic peaks, deep river canyons, thick forests, bald eagles, majestic stands of Giant Sequoia, open meadows, pristine alpine lakes, precarious hot mineral pools, swiftly flowing streams, cascades and rivers… of the most dramatic and breathtaking views of the Sierra Nevada mountain range — these are just a few of the natural wonders awaiting you as you travel the Ebbetts Pass National Scenic Byway."

The reason we took this road? It may have been the route chosen by William Henry to reach California from Carson City. This is my best guess; my great-great-grandfather did not inform Sarah in his letters to her of his route, unfortunately.

The mountains were rugged, punctuated by enormous giant boulders, conifers reaching the sky but blocking the possible trails that may have been forged over the range. It was a beautiful drive and as we climbed and then descended, we imagined what it must have been like for the early emigrants to traverse this land. "Impossible to believe" is one sentiment we shared. Another thought: These people were courageous and determined to reach the land of gold.

We were in the lap of automotive luxury as we glided through the mountains. The emigrants, who had just crossed the forty-mile desert, were rundown, ragged, half-starved—and yet they persevered. We could not conceive of a wagon making it over this range of mountains, no matter the route.

And there were several different routes to choose from. In 1846 the Donner Party went north of Lake Tahoe. Carson Pass is south of the lake. There was another cutoff further north and one further south. These paths had been used for centuries by the Native Americans. They knew the way. The early emigrants did not know the way. Historical accounts mention that many emigrants were helped by the Native Americans who acted as guides. But upon reaching the base of the mountains, they slipped away to let the emigrants forge their own way. Gazing up at the mountains from Carson City, I might have been one to decide that Carson Valley was good enough for me.

Carson City was a Mormon outpost that was established in 1851 because it was a good area for farming hay and grain. By 1861 the town's population stood at 500 people. It may be inferred that most gold miners did not stay in the Carson City area. A Mr. Abe Curry saw to it that Carson City was named the permanent capital of Nevada Territory. In October of 1864, Nevada became a state and

Carson City because the permanent state
capitol. Mr. Curry donated the land to the
state of Nevada for the capital building. Fun
fact: It was named after Kit Carson who never
stepped a foot in the town his entire life.

So off we went on highway 50. Once we
arrived at the vicinity of Bear Lake, we saw a
sign for Placerville, so we serendipitously took
the road less traveled. That road dropped us
down from almost 8,000 feet to the foothills at
about 1,000 feet. Our ears popped several
times. And this was a good reminder that the
emigrants made this leg of their journey at
very high elevation, which made the going that
much more difficult because everything is
more extreme.

Placerville was originally known as
Hangtown because five men were hanged from
the same tree for crimes committed. The town
was in the center of the Mother Lode gold
fields, so it grew quickly. The townspeople
favored a less morbid name and Placerville
competed with Colusa for that honor. Colusa

lost.

Our travel came to an end as we entered the driveway of our friends the Coverts, who live in West Sacramento about fifty miles from Placervlle. The night was filled with lively conversation and lots of catch-up visiting.

We made it in our day and age, just as William Henry had made it in his. The gold we found as result of our travels? Wonderful memories and a deep appreciation for the man who made this journey in 1850 and changed the course of his family's life forever. Sarah was deeply appreciated as well. Giving birth to all the children back then was no easy task. She was as much responsible as William Henry was in shaping the family's future. Her contribution was vital in every way and especially so by staying behind and providing love and direction for the children. As you will learn, the children would have their own trip of discovery.

CHAPTER SIX:
RETURNING TO BELOIT

Most of the letters that William Henry wrote informed Sarah about his activities in "Cala." After deciding that gold was not going to be his salvation, he turned his sights to farming. He leased some land and grew alfalfa, I am assuming, for hay. This opened him up to the weather, as is does with all farmers, and sometimes the weather provided and sometimes it didn't. To fill the gap, he farmed cauliflower and strawberries.

I had a hard time reconciling his farming success with money he was sending to Beloit. Seemed to me in reading his letters that he was always apologizing to Sarah for not sending much. And some research suggested that he continued to mine for gold while planting rows and rows of cauliflower and the like.

William Henry continued to farm in California on leased land and became convinced that this would be his lot in life. He also fell in love with the place. The weather pleased him as he described to Sarah, in a letter dated Dec. 7, 1850: "You ask does Cala look as pleasant as I expected? Now personally all I know of Cala is this hill country which is delightful in the summer, and not cold in the winter, we have had a little snow but in 2 to 3 days it is nearly gone, a little ice, the sun shines warm like a warm April day we had 3 spells of rain 2 to 3 days each, we are expecting an open winter."

In this same letter he then requests the birthdates of each of his children, for he does not know their ages exactly and "it makes me feel unpleasantly when I think of it." As an aside, this does not surprise me, as many men don't know their children's birthdates in my family. My brother doesn't know those of his sons, and my Uncle Ralph never knew anyone's birthday but his own.

William Henry then announces in the same letter that his candle set his letter on fire and "so I must quit until morning." But there is

more, presumably written the next day. It is a
letter packed with much information that
would be pertinent to those contemplating the
trip west.

Surprising to me, he reports that he read in
the New Orleans papers that "elder Springer is
dead and Lucy Hatch is married." Then asks if
George Woodward of Beloit has been killed by
a horse running away? Made me wonder about
newspapers from New Orleans arriving in the
foothills of California in 1850. Never imagined
anything like that so I googled it and
discovered the following:

After the 1848 Gold Rush, the Post Office
Department awarded a contract to the Pacific
Mail Steamship Company to transport mail to
California. During this time some mail was
carried by the military between Fort
Leavenworth and Santa Fe. The Overland Mail
Company stage line of John Butterfield was
also awarded a contract. The stages used the
2,800 mile southern route between Tipton,
Missouri, and San Francisco, California were

specified as a 24-day run but often it took months. Californians felt their isolation from lack of regular mail so a better idea was needed.[21]

In this same letter, William Henry offers his advice for those thinking of making the trip west.

"I think there were 6,000 families that immigrated here this year. People will cross the plains very safe and quick with mules but they are very dear and will not fetch much here and horses less.

"A snug built pony shaped milling sized horse is the best horse but oxen are safer and more profitable than horses and if properly managed nearly as

---

[21] U.S. Department of Transportation, Federal Highway Administration www.fhwa.dot.gov/infrastructure/back0304.cfm

quick on the whole better than mules or horses but cows are quicker than oxen will [make] the journey in less time, safer, in a few days equally as handy and the most profitable of all by far many tried them this year and without a dissenting voice preferred by all who tried them, a wagon that weighs more than five hundred is too heavy for oxen or cows, box cover & everything if much immigration next year horse and mules will be worth from $20 to $40, cows from $50 to $100, a horse wagon for 3 men and 4 horses should not exceed 400 lb."

He sounds like a travel agent circa 1850. Advising about wagons rather than train tickets and airplanes. Or maybe a Mayflower Moving Company van would be a more apt comparison.

Upon arriving back in the area of Beloit, he finds Sarah suffering from tuberculosis, and his children are now the following ages:

- Albert was 14
- Charles was 11
- Emma was 8
- William Orlando was 6
- Julia Mariah Dresser 12/19/1850[22]

---

[22] This meant that Julia was conceived just before William Henry left Beloit. And it also meant that the first time he saw her was upon his return in 1853. She was a toddler.

SAILING AWAY

1851   NORTHERN LIGHT   VANDERBILT

"There are a lot of mysterious things about boats, such as why anyone would get on one voluntarily."

-P.J. O'ROURKE

Having his family in Wisconsin territory and state for three years during his absence wore on William Henry and he finally decided to return to his family to make a decision on their future. And to do this, he booked passage on steamships from San Francisco to New York City via Panama.

So how was that possible? The Panama Canal did not exist. Research unearths the following information from the Smithsonian (paraphrased):

For Easterners, sailing to and from the gold fields was a dangerous and stormy voyage. Vessels sailed around Cape Horn at the southern tip of South America, some 14,000 miles in all. It took roughly 200 days. Wealthier travelers could save months by boarding steamships for Panama and Nicaragua. There, they crossed through tropical jungles to the Pacific Coast to catch ships bound for San Francisco. (This was also true in the opposite direction.)

Another interesting tidbit was that a train was built for the travelers to transit Panama.

Before the train was completed, the traveler was forced to pay the ever-rising price for a trip in a dugout canoe to Las Cruces, Panama. The train tracks were completed in January 1855 by private U.S.companies using private funds. William Henry crossed Panama in 1853.

And so it happened that William Henry made the trip and utilized the dugout canoe to reach the other side of Panama in order to complete his journey to New York. I have also concluded that he was at this point, "wealthier." Finally, I discovered that he boarded the *Cortes,* from San Francisco some time after July 13th and he sailed into NY Harbor on the *Northern Light* on August 24, 1853. One trip, two ships (and don't forget the canoe!).

Quite an adventure, slogging through the Panamanian jungle to avoid Cape Horn. Upon reaching New York, he took a few days to get back to Beloit.

Unfortunately, Rayman and I have decided

not to do that part of his trip because the Panama Canal was built and there is no way to re-create the trip adequately. I asked my friends Dick and Karen Watts if they would sail me to Panama from Morro Bay on their boat. They laughed. So did I.

Once William Henry was back in Beloit, the letters, of course, stopped. I haven't found out how he filled his time. I'm guessing he farmed and helped rear the children.

A very short and meaningful life was snuffed out when Sarah died on the 23rd of May, 1854. Tuberculosis had its way with her. Records call her disease consumption, but it was likely tuberculosis. People in the 1800s may have regarded tuberculosis like cancer…a dreaded disease. It took until the mid-1900s for a medical treatment that saved people from dying from the bacterial disease according to American Lung Association.

As I stated earlier, Rayman and I couldn't find her grave when we visited the cemetery where Sarah's family (the Jenks) are interred.

We know she wasn't cremated as that technology was not used until later. This leaves me with more questions than answers.

We know, however, that William Henry returned to California after Sarah died. A paper trail left by my great grandfather, William Orlando, was recorded in a book featuring San Luis Obispo history, and revealed this information about William Henry.[23]

The aforementioned book (*History of San Luis Obispo*) reports that after returning to the East, (my great-great-grandfather)[William Henry] had California on his mind and in "1860, returns with his family by once again making the cross country trek starting out in 1859, the fall, he and his party left Rockford,

[23] Morrison, Annie L. *History of San Luis Obispo and Environs, California: With Biographical Sketches of Leading men and Women of the County and Environs Who Have Been Identified With the Growth and Development of the Section from the Early Days to the Present,* Historic Record Company, Los Angeles, California, 1917.

IL, driving their horses and wagons as far as the Pawnee river, Fort Scott, Kansas, where they wintered until the following spring. They then started in reality to cross the plains, using oxen and cows to draw wagons, outfitting once or twice between the Republican river and the Platte, when they lost part of their equipment. At length they struck the overland trail and arriving in the Golden State, settled in Yolo county."[24]

And that is how this branch of the Dresser family's life was shaped by making an effort and by taking on tremendous risk.

It was great fun to take the route William Henry used to California. With that trip in our rearview mirror, we returned to Portland, Oregon where I continued to record the history of the Dresser family.

---

[24] *Lanctot, Heather,* Archives & Records Center Coordinator, Yolo County Archives & Records Center, Woodland, CA, Dec. 2, 2021 email. 226 Buckeye Street, Woodland, CA 95695

The Second Generation Settles in California

I have had enough experience in all my years, and have read enough of the past, to know that advice to grandchildren is usually wasted. If the second and third generations could profit by the experience of the first generation, we would not be having some of the troubles we have today.

HARRY TRUMAN

In 1860, my great-grandfather, William Orlando Dresser, was a teenager of about thirteen years of age. His oldest brother, Albert, was around twenty. And the middle brother was about eighteen. Traveling with his children must have made the trip so much better for William Henry, who by this time was about forty-seven. The kids surely helped saddle up the horses, lead the livestock to water and the like. Those young men were big and strong. Having said that, the journey had become more dangerous because the Native Americans were losing their patience with the emigrants—as you might well imagine (and the facts of history tell us). [25]

---

[25] Ages are approximate because exact dates are unknown.

CHAPTER SEVEN:
YOLO LAND

For those who have not had the pleasure of visiting Yolo County, it is located in the northwestern part of California. Yolo was where the Dressers decided to settle.

Once arrived, William Henry acquired land. So did his son, William Orlando Dresser, when old enough to do so. This land they purchased was transferred under the instrument called a patent. As a Yolo Historical Society member explained,

"Patents are a form of land granting that the United States Federal government did throughout the 1800s. Patents are legal documents issued by the federal government that grant an individual the title to land that is held by the government. The patents of public lands could be purchased by, or

donated to, private owners. One reason that land was donated was for military service. Patents were also made to encourage westward expansion."

The researchers who helped me discovered that William Orlando Dresser received his first patent in Yolo County in 1867 when he was just 20 years old. He then started selling off property in 1877, and by 1880 he was living in Stanislaus County, in the San Joaquin Valley of California. He owned multiple properties around Dunnigan and Zamora, some apparently for only a brief period.[26]

Of interest is that the Dressers lived in Paradise, California for a time. Becky Dresser's arm of the family remained in Paradise and had worked to preserve records in the local museum. Unfortunately, all was lost when the

---

[26] In total, the Dressers, both father and son, took possession of 860 acres over relatively short period of time.

town was burnt to the ground in November of 2018. The Feather River flowed through this area and William Henry returned to that river to mine while living in the area.

William Henry and William Orlando also lived in Grafton, California, as evidenced by the U.S. Census of 1870. In 1880 the census lists William Henry as a resident of Santa Ana, California having moved there for health reasons. William Henry Dresser died in Santa Ana on September 7, 1894.

The people in the Yolo historical group discovered not only the property, but also the fact that William Orlando had moved to Stanislaus by 1880. He must have parlayed his money and purchased property in the Central Valley and then Paso Robles (a town on the Central Coast).

Before William Orlando left Yolo County, he married Mary Rickey in Sacramento, California, in 1875. They then moved to the San Joaquin Valley.

William Orlando Dresser

Mary Rickey Dresser

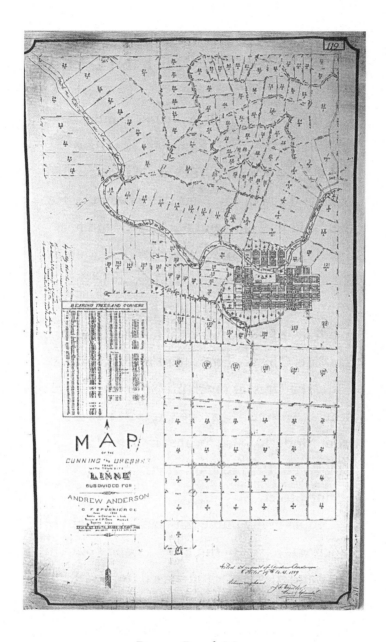

Dresser Ranch Map

214 | From Beloit to Clark Gable

CHAPTER EIGHT:
PASO ROBLES COMES INTO VIEW

When the family of William Orlando
relocated from Yolo County to Stanislaus
County 1879/1880, William Orlando farmed
grain and alfalfa and ran a dairy business. He
then sold that land and purchased land near
Snelling, California, in the county of Merced.
Grain and cattle were his endeavors in that
location. It was in 1882 that he purchased a
ranch near Paso Robles, California, County of
San Luis Obispo. From 1882 through at least
1894, the Dresser ranch property was leased to
others. Around 1894, the Dressers relocated
from Modesto (also located in Stanislaus
County) to Paso Robles. Their home was on
Spring Street.

People in my immediate family thought the
ranch was a part of the Eureka Land Grant in
1882 and that it was purchased from a Mr. Jim
Jones. This version remains unverified. There
was no Eureka Land Grant. The ranch was part

of the Ascensions Land Grant, according to research done by the Paso Robles Area Historical Society.

my home people.

A BARGAIN FOR A LIFE TIME

*PR Record
July 20,
1912
p. 4*

The beautiful 154 acre chicken ranch for sale, known as the Dr Dresser ranch and one of the finest fitted up poultry ranches in the state; water piped to all grounds and buildings of which there is 60, all No. 1. All implements and machinery goes with the place. At present stocked with upwards of 2000 laying hens. 25 acres alfalfa. Large pumping plant and reservoir. 40 acres summer-fallow for wheat or barley everytning goes except chickens and they can be bought cheap. $50.00 per acre will buy this grand property. Apply to
C. D. ASHBAUGH,
Paso Robles, Cal.
Sole Agent for same.

If you look closely at the map on page 213, you will notice that it mentions Dunning and Dresser. You will notice also the township of Linne. This was the vision of people at that time. Subdividing it was brilliant because when the ranch was sold in the 1970s, it was subdivided from this document.

The only things that existed were the listed oak trees and the brick house, and the planned town of Linne. The location, which was once a stagecoach stop and post office and perhaps hotel, was too far from the railroad and so it was never developed as envisioned.

The Dresser ranch was referred to as the Dunning and Dresser ranch on the subdivision map, yet its origins remain a bit hazy. My uncle, Ralph Dresser, reported to me that the ranch was purchased in 1882. It was originally 7,000 acres. Four thousand acres were sold "later on." My uncle also told me that Shetland ponies were raised on the ranch and grain was the main crop. Further, the Paso Robles Area Historical Society found a "for sale" ad in the local paper of July 20, 1912 for a 154 acre chicken business located at the ranch.[27] See previous page.

Mr. Lorenzo Dunning strategically married

[27] Paso Robles Record, July 20, 1912, page 4.

Julia Dresser, the sister of William Orlando
Dresser, in Yolo County in November, 1869.
He, too, owned land in Yolo County. Lorenzo
Dunning sold his acreage at some point and
moved to the San Joaquin Valley, as did
William Orlando. That they become co-owners
doesn't surprise. The reason Dunning sold out
is unknown. Since he lived in the San Joaquin
Valley, perhaps he wanted property closer to
home. This is unsubstantiated speculation by
this great-granddaughter.

Meanwhile, William Orlando and Mary
were busy with small children, which was
probably the deciding factor in regard to living
on Spring Street (aka "in town"). Their home
was located at 1735 Spring Street in Paso
Robles. There is scant information about
Mary. She had the children and as a mother,
was quite busy. They employed a "helper" but
I don't have a name and I don't know if that
person was a live-in helper or not. Again I
lament that women get lost in history.

William Orlando, in addition to plowing up

fields at the ranch, plowed into local politics.
He was the mayor of the budding little town.
And when on the board for the town, voted in
a new "sewer" system. It allowed certain
buildings to hook up to the system which
allowed raw sewage to flow down to the
Salinas River. The following is a newspaper
article proclaiming the vote on February 1,
1904.[28] He also served on the school board.
June of that year, my Great Aunt Nellie
graduated from the high school with six other
seniors.[29] Paso was still a small town.

[28] The Paso Robles Record, June 4, 1904.

[29] pasoroblesdailynews.com/looking-back-to-1904-
seven-students-graduate-from-paso-robles-high-
school/145079/

General Land Office.

GEO. W. STEWART, Register.

ORDINANCE NO. 93.

IN RELATION TO THE CONNECTING OF
PRIVATE SEWERS AND DRAINS WITH
THE SEWER SYSTEM OF THE CITY
OF EL PASO DE ROBLES

The Board of Trustees of the City of El Paso
de Robles do ordain as follows:

SECTION—1—Every House, and building
connecting with the Sewer System of the City
of El Paso de Robles, must be governed by the
provisions of Ordinance 89.

SEC—2—Before making any connection
with the sewer system of said City of El Paso
de Robles, for any private residence, house or
building, the owner or lessee thereof must pay
to the City Clerk of said City, the sum of Ten
dollars, for the priviledge of making such
connection, and any licensed drain layer making any connection without payment having
been first made as aforesaid, will be liable on
his bond for the amount.

SEC.—3—None of the provisions of Section
2 of this ordinance shall apply to property owners on the line of the sewer system of said City,
who have been assessed and have paid their
assessments for the construction of the main
sewer of said Sewer system.

SEC.—4—This ordinance shall be published twice in the LEADER, a weekly newspaper
printed, published and circulated in the City
of El Paso de Robles, and shall be in full force
and effect from and after its passage and ap-
proval

Introduced January 18th, 1904, and passed
Feb. 1st 1904 by the following vote:

Ayes;Trustees Brend.in, Dresser, Brooks.

Noes None,

Absent Monteith, Nelson.

Approved ebruary 1st 1904

T. BROOKS, President of the Board of Trustees

Attest L. E. WILLIAMS, Clerk.

In researching, I attempted to verify dates,
acreage, and the like. Being that it all

happened just thirty-two years after California achieved statehood, the records were sketchy and hard to find. This involved going to the Recorder's Office for the County of San Luis Obispo. Oh, my. It robbed me of all hope of settling the discussion by way of fact. Given that, I abandoned the effort of exactness so as not to bore myself or the reader any further.

The Dresser ranch was located approximately six miles east of Paso Robles. Linne Road leads the traveler into the property (if arriving off Niblick Road). Three thousand acres was what the Dressers eventually ended up with and that is what I will now address. They farmed barley, planted an almond orchard, and raised cattle. A chicken ranch and Shetland ponies were also a feature on the ranch at one time. Some people regarded the ranch as the best cattle ranch in the area.

It was a hard life, but they apparently made enough off the land to keep it and pay property taxes. One way they stayed afloat, as previously mentioned, was to lease some of the land for others to farm. This helped the Dressers considerably. The ranch had no mortgage when my mother's generation began selling off parcels.

William Orlando also got involved with oil and water. The ranch was mostly dry-farmed but he wanted to find water so they could irrigate the crops. This led him to drill. With the discovery of oil in San Ardo, which was just thirty five miles north, they also hoped for a gusher.

Jumping to the next generation for a moment, grandpa loved to drive out to the ranch when I lived with my grandparents. Surveying his property brought him great joy. He would check out the cattle that were shading up under the sprawling limbs of the live oak trees that grew all over the ranch. He would stop to get water from the spigot near the trough. What spigot, you ask? The family drilled for water in 1926 and were successful. Below is a picture of the event.

This was not the only drilling at the Dresser or Dunning and Dresser Ranch. According to reporting in the *Paso Robles Recorder*, Sept. 6, 1913, oil was suspected to be present "between the Her Hero and Estrella river, east of this city and all that [was] necessary was proper prospecting." The article continues, "Last week at a depth of 884 feet, oil sand was encountered which produced several gallons of the crude oil. The temperature at this depth was 109 degrees and at a depth of 850 feet the temperature rose to 120 degrees."

In the *Paso Robles Review* (dated November 15, 1913), another article appeared. This report stated, "Mr. F. Landreth of Los Angeles has been making preparations to pump the water from the well, and, with this in view has placed a two inch pump in operation. The object is to prove oil indication and make further prospects."

On November 22, 1913, the *Paso Robles Record* reported, "A pump was placed in the well by the Paso Robles Mercantile Co. the first of the week... During the progress of pumping oil was emitted from the well. The pump also disgorged small pieces of asphalt which, when mashed, bore strong indications of oil." This reporting indicated that people were very interested in finding oil in the area.

Work continued and a driller from the Taft and Coalinga district was engaged.

At this point, the fate of the well disappears from public accounts. However, on February 16, 1921, another article surfaces in the *Paso Robles Star*. This time Union Oil is implicated as having purchased some land at the Big Beckett property. Unable to find the Big

Beckett property today, I do not know how close to the Dresser ranch it was. Nothing else is mentioned until the *Paso Robles Times* reported on Feb. 22, 1936, that "there are three wells planned for the district east of here." Then the reporting dries up—if you'll pardon the pun.

Finally, another company drilled at the ranch. No oil was found, much to everyone's chagrin, but more water was. Therefore a spigot was installed next to the trough out at the ranch. The water brought out of the ground was exceptionally good and jugs were filled and brought back to Paso because Paso's water was not as good. So, the drilling did have a bright side. A few pictures and an old sign made of wood are the remains of the day. I'm sure when they were drilling, they must have spent time imagining life as rich people, not unlike those who currently play the lottery. You know, "What should we do with our money?" Turns out it was just a rhetorical question.

I can remember a derrick drilling at the ranch probably in the 1950s. It was very impressive especially when it was lit up. They must have drilled at night, hence the lights. This drilling was done where the spigot was but I cannot be certain if the earlier drilling or the drilling in the '50s found that water.

Moving along, I will now show how the family expanded and contracted. Next in chart form is the Dresser family lineage (my maternal side).

William Orlando Dresser and Mary Dresser

	Children:	Offspring:
Ralph (1877)	None	None
Joseph Irwin (1879)	None	None
Bertha (1882)	Bobby Freeman	Four
Nell (1886)	Billy Brewster	One
William Rollo (1888)	Donna Dresser	Two (me and my brother, John)
	William Ralph Dresser	None
Ruby (1892)	None	None
Wanda (1894)	None	None

The family chart also illustrates that a family of seven children, distilled down to my grandfather, William Rollo's generation to just four children and then those four children (my mother's generation), grew to seven children.

At this juncture, I pivot to the next generation, the generation of my grandfather,

William Rollo, who was born in Modesto in 1888. He was one of seven children.

Now it is time to meet these characters and find out what happened with this family and how it came to be that Clark Gable came to visit the ranch in the 1930s.

The Third Generation

William Orlando and his wife, my great-grandmother Mary, must have been instrumental in encouraging their sons and daughters to pursue certain lines of work. Irwin, the second oldest, was to be a banker. Ralph Dresser, the first born, was to be a doctor. And William Rollo, the youngest son, was to be the farmer/rancher. The daughters were encouraged to be educated in the field of nursing, and perhaps, business.

To add personalities to this mix, I will now introduce you to my "great" relatives, the children of William Orlando and Mary Dresser.

CHAPTER NINE:
RALPH ORLANDO DRESSER

The oldest child of William Orlando and Mary Dresser was Ralph Orlando Dresser, born in Yolo County in 1876. After graduating from high school in Paso Robles, he applied to study medicine at the University of California, Berkeley. His father routinely wrote him letters while he was in college. Some of the letters still exist and they impart interesting information of the times. The letters were mailed to Ralph Dresser, Berkeley, CA. That's it. No street address. No zip code. (Of course, zip codes weren't a thing back then). Hard to believe in this day and age that he ever received the letters.

There is an example of father to son on the next page.

Paso Robles Dec 8 - 99

Dear Ralph. - We arrived home from Tulare Tues Evening. Had good weather and fine roads. Found all quite well at Uncle Alberts. The only thing that marred the trip a little was the horse ("Ned") got sick on the way home, so that he could hardly travel. We came near laying out all night in the desert but managed to reach — Dudleys quite a while after dark. The next day we only made 18 miles reached Cholame at 1 oclock but Ned was so weak he could go no further so we laid over till next day and reached home Tues instead of monday night. The horse is getting all right again. Found all well at home. Ray is still with us but hasn't struck

We started home Saturday.

This letter captures how long it took to cross from Tulare to Paso Robles in 1899.

There were also letters written to his son with two different addresses in San Francisco. One address was on Taylor Street, and the other on Gough. Having recently visited both, I don't think the buildings currently at these addresses are the original buildings. The 1906 earthquake would have been the reason for that, perhaps

After graduating in 1901, Ralph came back to Paso Robles and practiced medicine in the tiny town. He had an office in the Acorn building at the corner of 13th and Park Street. It may have been one of several locations he used as his office over the twenty-five or so years he practiced medicine.

Phil Dirkz, a noted Paso Robles columnist for the local newspaper, wrote that Dr. Dresser once amputated a thumb of a Walt Freeman, who was nine years old at the time. Young Walt had wrapped his thumb with the rope around the horn of his saddle. With no hospitals at that time, the family came into town for the medical treatment. With a few whiffs of ether, the thumb was taken.

On November 1, 1922, the *Paso Robles Star* reported that "Dr's Kelker and Dr. Dresser sealed secrets of the operating room in an operation performed on Walter Hughes who was suddenly taken ill. There being no time to rush him to the hospital, the doctors borrowed a Mexican machete from an erstwhile Madero revolutionist, and laying the victim on an ironing board removed, amidst much pain and many groans, an immense apple from his interior. The patient recovered immediately and remained to enjoy the evening."

This reporting leaves me a bit confused but I love the machete and the ironing board. Quite a visual.

Doc Dresser was married, which came as a complete surprise to me. He died before I was born but there were family discussions whenever his name came up but I do not remember anyone discussing his wife. I discovered his marriage through the U.S. Census records. He married a woman named

Madeline whom had a daughter by a previous
marriage and they employed a young woman
for domestic help. He and Madeline lived in
the house at 503 13th Street in Paso Robles,
which they purchased from Oscar Claassen.
That house was built in 1919.

In 1925, Doc Dresser became ill with acute
pain on his left side. He decided to take the
train to San Francisco for possible surgery.
Unfortunately, his appendix burst. You see, the
appendix was on his left side, not the usual
right side of his body and it was told to me
that he was unsure about the origin of pain.
Hence, the train trip. He died in San Francisco
in 1925. He was forty-nine years old.

Doctor Dresser's wife outlasted him and
died in San Francisco in November, 1932. Her
sister, Gertrude Le Vey, of San Francisco,
arranged for her funeral. The couple had no
children of their own.

With all the family pictures I have, I regret
to report that I don't have one of him… or her,
with one possible exception. Since I can't

verify it, I will let the matter rest here.

It should also be mentioned that members of the Dresser family traveled the state and took great interest in property. Next is a letter that Ralph Orlando wrote to Rollo, my grandfather.

Berkeley. Apr. 30. - 1907,

Dear Rollo. - I am,
here yesterday afternoon. Found Ella
feeling quite poorly from a billious
spell and uncle Ren not feeling
any too well. The rest about as usual. I left home the fore part of
last week and stopped off at Sunnyvale
to look round a little for a day or
two. Sunnyvale is a new town
just started and they are trying
to make a manufacturing town of
it. So I made a little investment
there in a couple of business lots
at $1725. Each or 3450 ly it was
a pretty good price but it seemed
to me that the town has a future
and if so we ought to make a little

and girls — There are 20 trains a day passing the town Each way making 40 trains in all. The 1st of this month contracts were let for 50ty houses, and others are building as fast as they can get men and material. There is so much more life there than in Paso Robles that it seemed good to me to see something going on so took a chance with the town. I got as near the center as I could get; just across the street and a few steps north of the Bank Building. The P.R. Co has made the town a terminal point. Which is quite an item in fright rates. — Well Rollo I see you are quite interested in the Cigar store. When I arr. here yesterday found your two letters awaiting me and also rec'd one of the 28th this morning and I would be only too glad to help you out but don't see how we could take hold of any thing of that kind at present

over

Quite an amazing idea regarding Sunnyvale, California in hindsight!

CHAPTER TEN:
GREAT UNCLE
JOSEPH IRWIN DRESSER

My grandfather's other brother (the one who was to become a banker) also died young. He was found dead on the Dresser ranch. His name was Joseph Irwin Dresser and he was a very good bicycle rider, as was my Uncle Ralph. See page 332. He was born in 1879.

Below is some information about his demise. It was suicide. Depression existed (and exists) in our family.

"Paso Robles, Sept. 24, 1898

Irvin Dresser, twenty years old, shot himself near this city this morning. The body was found by a party of small boys with a revolver near his side, with a bullet in the right temple. He lived four hours after being discovered. He was a son of City Councilman W.O. Dresser, and highly respected."

Another account of the death the following day is as follows:

"Last evening the TRIBUNE received by telephone the sad intelligence of the death of Irving Dresser, who died at his home in Paso Robles at 5 o'clock from a bullet wound in the head.

"The information received at this office was that the deceased had been ill for

some time but on the morning of this sad occurrence he was feeling better and in company with his little brother, procured a gun, and with a revolver upon his person they left Paso Robles for a short stroll through the hills. After roaming around for some time they came to the Sand Springs, where they sat down to rest. A short time afterward Dresser's little brother arose and said, 'I'm going home' and walked away, thinking that his brother would soon follow, but he did not.

"About 3 o'clock in the afternoon Mr. A.B. Gill, who resides near the Sand Springs, came into Paso Robles and reported that he had seen a dead man near the springs.

"Justice C.H. Arnold in company with Y.B. Sanders, B.B. Pierce and others immediately left for the scene of the tragedy. Upon their arrival at the springs they found young Irving Dresser lying prostrate upon the ground with a bullet hole in his head near the right temple. He was yet alive.

"The wounded man was taken to his home, where Dr. J.H. Glass made a search for the bullet but could not locate it. At 5 o'clock Dresser breathed his last.

"Deceased was the son of W.O. Dresser, and 19 years of age. He was a member of the senior class of the Paso Robles High school, a bright pupil and a general favorite among his associates.

"A coroner's jury was summoned and viewed the remains, after which they adjourned until Monday morning at 9 o'clock when the inquest will be held. "The grief stricken family have the sympathy of the entire community."

In reviewing letters Irwin wrote to his brother, Ralph, he displayed good penmanship, a gift for learning (he was valedictorian of his class), a good leader as the President of the class. Also known as a hard worker, he wrote to Ralph,

"Would you like to work in harvesting. I have got a job on the little ranch with Biz and Dooley. I was going to load both (word I can't make out) wagons for $1.50 a day and Biz said he has to have another boy drive 3 horses only two lines(?). He was only going to give

you $1.25 and I told him to split the difference and give us $1.25 a piece and said alright. It is only a ten foot header and we can change about how we work. I can load one day and you the next. The job will only last about 20 days and you can make about $25. If you want to work you must let me know at once as Biz wants to know. Just take your choice you can work or not work."

Fast forward to 2021, while looking for an appliance manual in my paper files (what are the chances?), I found this clipping from the Tribune, dated July 4, 1898, just two months before he died:

■ ■ ■

Big bicycle race

PASO ROBLES — Cyclists are greatly excited over the coming Fourth of July meet. Harry Downing, the professional champion of the coast, and Bunt Smith, who recently broke the world's five-mile record, time 9.01, both of San Jose, are intending to be here and take part in the racing.

Irvin Dresser, the county champion in the professional class, is in fine shape and is confident of winning the medal for the third and last time.

The five-mile race, professional, will cause a great deal of interest owing to the event being paced by a triplet manned by three crack professionals. Paul Smith is the favorite in the amateur class.

As the Sacramento and Paso Robles meets are the only ones in the State on the Fourth, it is expected that our neighboring towns will send their best representatives.

■ ■ ■

An amazing find where I least expected it.

To extend the Dresser family tree, let me introduce you to my grandfather's sisters.

CHAPTER ELEVEN:
GREAT AUNT
BERTHA DRESSER FREEMAN

Aunt Bertha was a gem. She trained as a nurse in the Bay Area; obviously, she was smart, strong, clever, hardworking, and sweet.

If you consider it, going north like that (from a rural outpost like Paso Robles at the time to the "big city" of San Francisco) as a single woman to study was quite impressive in those days. And that's what she did.

Great Aunt Bertha married a man named Mollie Holtz Freeman, who hailed from Palo Pinto County, Texas. The Dresser family was reportedly not keen on the match, but did not prevent it. Mollie leased some land at the Dresser ranch. As previously mentioned, Bertha had studied nursing in San Francisco and that came in handy the day the horse Mollie was riding stepped in a squirrel hole. The horse fell on top of Mollie and paralyzed him from the waist down. That didn't stop Mollie from getting around. He learned to drive his car by using sticks on the gas and brake pedals.

Mollie and Bertha, too, spent time living out at the ranch in the old stagecoach stop/post office which was referred to as the two-story brick house. A regular visitor to the house was a doctor who traveled up and down the state. As luck would have it, the doctor was an artist and painted fine murals on the upstairs hall or in the stairwell leading to the second floor. I do not remember ever seeing the murals. And there are no pictures of the murals.

Anyway, back to Great Aunt Bertha. And

Great Uncle Mollie. They lived in that house until Mollie died, reportedly while wheel-chairing himself down the sidewalk in town where he had a heart attack. So Great Aunt Bertha did what was to become a family habit, packing up a few belongings and leaving the house for good. She left dishes on the table. And just walked away. That was May 10, 1947. Mollie was fifty-five years old. She then moved to Great Aunt Wanda's house on Spring Street.

Bertha and Mollie's only son, Bobby, had by this time married his wife, Donna. When they married in 1946, they lived in the house at 1 Dresser Place... the house many others lived in over the years.

There the brick house sat vacant until young buckaroos convinced themselves that gold was hidden in the floors—and the ransacking began. The gold rumors are ironic given that William Henry came to California for gold but could not make a living at it. The house was near a place where the young local men got themselves "liquored up," and so the house (which should have been preserved as a historic monument) burned to the ground. And where was Great Aunt Bertha? In town, living with her sister Wanda.

David Skinner, a Paso Roblan of some renown, wrote about the old hotel. Here is the link: **pasorobles-usa.com/hotel.htm**

Bobby Freeman, Great Aunt Bertha's son, sold insurance, many times, out of his car. He was also a grain buyer for California Milling Corp. He loved to drink. Donna, his wife, loved to drink. So this killed any relationship with my grandmother. She already had a husband who drank too much. She was not in the mood to expand her close friendships with them, family or not.

And while I lived in the same town as the Freemans, I saw them about as much as if they had lived on Doros Island off Athens in the Aegean Sea. This I now regret.

The Freemans beat feet to Paso Robles proper and lived at 402 Oak Street when Donna became pregnant with my cousin Sharon (my second cousin) in 1949. Then when their child Rick was born, they moved to 1728 Spring Street, across Spring Street from Aunt Wanda. Their final move landed them on Trejo Lane, on the other side of the Salinas River.

A funny aside. My grandmother didn't get along with her sisters-in-law too well. Particularly Wanda. But Bertha was her favorite. When my grandmother got around to spiffing up her new house (at 1612 Oak Street), she bought some wallpaper for the bathroom. It was stuck on the wall facing the porcelain throne, aka toilet. Different scenes were depicted on that wallpaper. An old claw bath tub with duck feet instead of lion's paws. A tub with a shower curtain all around and three arms sticking out the top. Another scene featured a long rectangular mirror with four shaving mugs. Each mug had a name: Harry, Tom, Dick... and Bertha. Bertha's portion of the mirror was smashed. This cracked me up. Loved that wallpaper. Not sure if Aunt Bertha ever saw it... but it was very funny. Mel Brooks may have designed it!

I don't know if it's true, but I don't think any of the Dresser women drove. This impression was also held by my cousin Sharon. I never saw them driving. So Bobby Freeman and grandpa (every so often) took care of them. They bought their groceries, ran their errands. When my grandfather died, Bobby took care of affairs on the ranch as well as looking after the sisters. According to Uncle Ralph (William Ralph Dresser), Bobby took

liberties with the income from the ranch.
Everyone was still splitting everything.
Bobby's alleged shenanigans gave my uncle
some leverage because my uncle wanted to sell
the ranch. Bobby didn't. Uncle Ralph had an
audit conducted privately, and more or less
suggested that if Bobby didn't agree to sell, he
would turn over the auditor's findings to the
authorities. Bobby's choice. Bobby agreed to
sell. This is, of course, an abbreviated version
of a story that involved lots of angst.

CHAPTER TWELVE:
GREAT AUNT NELL DRESSER BREWSTER

I never knew Great Aunt Nell. It was Great Aunt Nell who invested in a stationery shop on 13th Street across from the park in Paso Robles. She was a kind person. I'm told.

It is unclear how she met and married her husband, Clarence. He was born in San Luis Obispo county in 1883. Other information has not been forthcoming.

I discovered that my cousin, Sharon Freeman Kelly, had a treasure trove of old letters that were written by Great Aunt Nell's husband. Clarence was quite a go-getter, traveling between Los Angeles and San Francisco in search of ways to make money. On December 6, 1916, he wrote Nell a letter telling her of his business success and, oh, by the way, his plans to travel to Kentucky and on his way home to spend significant time in Oregon and Washington.

In August 1917, he wrote to inform Nell
that he was on the steamship *Yale* traveling to
San Francisco. In December, he wrote Nell and
mentioned Billy. Billy was their son. There
were no letters indicating a baby was in the
works.

William Dresser Brewster, the son of
Clarence and Nell, was born on November 17,
1917. The last letter from Clarence was dated
in May, 1917. Then in October 1918, the
telegram arrived announcing his death on
October 25, 1918. He died at Mare Island,
near San Francisco, of pneumonia.

Nell and baby Billy had been living with her
parents (William Orlando and Mary Dresser)
on Spring Street in Paso Robles as Clarence
moved about the country digging up business.
When Clarence died unexpectedly, Great Aunt
Wanda had Nell and baby Billy move into her
house and she helped rear Billy. She was much
more involved in Nell's life than I ever knew.
Unfortunately, Great Aunt Nell died on
February 18, 1947 at age 52 of breast cancer

and is buried in the Paso Robles cemetery.

Billy inherited her share of everything and spent it on wine, women, and song. He was a bit of character. It was said you really couldn't rely on him for anything except check-cashing. He married a woman named Elsie from Oklahoma. They had a son, Billy Junior. Elsie had a daughter, Janet, from a previous marriage. Billy Junior was a chip off the old block who never amounted to much. He never had any offspring, so that limb of the family stopped with him. Great Aunt Wanda told Billy Senior that he should not adopt his stepdaughter, Janet, or he would be disinherited. Pretty cruel but that was Aunt Wanda. I say it was pretty cruel, however, I did not know when I first started researching that Wanda helped rear Billy after Clarence died. Billy Junior waited until Great Aunt Wanda died, and then adopted Janet. He died on March 10, 1975.

CHAPTER THIRTEEN:
GREAT AUNT SADIE WANDA DRESSER WARDEN

Great Aunt Wanda (pictured above, fourth from the left) was quite often in bed. This is my recollection of her. It was rumored that she had a bad heart. She married Roy Warden, who was from a storied family of San Luis Obispo. For more information about the Wardens, I refer you to this website: occgs. com/projects/rescue/family_files/files/

WARDEN Family.pdf. By the time I entered this world, the two had divorced.

The thing about Great Aunt Wanda was she was always involved with affairs of the ranch. I can remember family meetings about ranch business when I was too young to understand the import of such conversations. My grandmother did not get along with Wanda very well. She was my grandmother's least favorite sister-in-law, I think it fair to say. She was, however, a very loyal family member. Opening her home to her widowed sisters and the son of sister Nell, who had died young, was a profoundly generous act. I liked all my great aunts, including Great Aunt Wanda. She gave me a $100 check for my freshman year of college. I loved her for that—and for her piano playing. She had the gift of hearing a song and then playing it without music. A rare gift indeed.

Looking back, it is sad that she and her sisters rarely visited my grandparents' house, which was only about two blocks away. Of course, what I remembered as a child was not much since I was distracted by my own circumstances, plus the fact that most young people are so self-absorbed that family stories are not on the top ten list for attention.

Great Aunt Wanda never had children of her own but she did have little Billy, Nell's son, to supervise and help. I think she was under-appreciated by my grandmother.

CHAPTER FOURTEEN:
GREAT AUNT
RUBY DRESSER CUMMINGS

Ruby was a beauty and rumor had it that
Frank Cummings married her on a dare. True?
Not sure but it makes a great story. Some
letters he wrote to her while he was out of
town hint at another story. He addresses one

"To Mine Darlin Prudence."

In this letter, he sounds smitten.

Mine darlin Prudence,

    What do you think Peaches I got me a job. Now
do not get too excited,its a bum one,no money,no business
no nothin.Roy and Goodwin had to go to the City today
and I am running the joint.Do you know I think I would
g t fat on a job like this if someone would furnish
the eats.
    I thought sure I would get a letter from you
this morning.Did you not say Birdie wrote to her dear
husband every other day.And I have not heard from you
for a week.You are cruel to me.
    I expect to get the car today on the way home.
I wish I had it down here now for it would be a good
chance to shine it up,but I guess I will not be so
busy tomorrow and then I can give it a good one.
    Are you having a nice visit with everyone? And
am I missing some parties.Well so are you.Roy and I
have one every night,feed and everything,and if you
all do not hurry and come home we are going to become
desperate and go to a show.Then you will be sorry and
envy us when we tell you how good it was.
    Gee I am excited I just had a customer. He wanted
to trade in a bicycle and a hundred dollars on a big
Cadillac.The transation ended when I found out that all
he really had was the bicycle and that he expected the
hundred in a few days.I told him to go out and hold up
the bank then I would talk turkey to him.So if you hear
of a bank being robbed blame me.
    Have you any prospects of a ride up or am I expect
ed down to get you?We are all out of eats now and I do
not know what to do.Shall I buy some more or what? I
might hold out for a few days and live on grass but I
do not want to turn into that kind of a contented cow.
    Do you miss me?
            Love,

This will conclude my daily report.Hope to be on again
tomorrow if I hear from you.Signing off till then.

Turns out that Great Aunt Ruby married
one of the smartest businessmen in town. He
owned the Park Pharmacy, located in the old
Acorn building across from the park, located in

the middle of town. And just a few doors west of my grandfather's pool parlor. While my grandfather was farming, and hoisting cars at the gas station, and playing snooker and poker, "Uncle Dodo" (this nickname for him is probably from his signature above, which appears to be "Doad") was busy running the drugstore, designing my grandparents' house on Oak Street, and other things I don't know of. Frank was very successful and bought one of the grandest houses in Paso Robles at the time. They lived at 1045 Olive Street. The house looked as though it had been flown in from Alabama. Two stories, stately white columns framing the front door, a green house, a fish pond, tiled kitchen (when linoleum was all the rage), beautiful banister leading to the second floor. In researching this house, I discovered there were just four rooms according the spec sheet I found. The wainscoting was mahogany. There was also a basement and that is where his will was lost, according to my grandmother. But I'm getting ahead of myself.

This house was built by Dr. Summerset Robinson in 1885. The house sat vacant from 1886 until 1916 when the Weed family bought it. Frank Cummings then bought it and lived there with Great Aunt Ruby until his death on March 25, 1956.

The house came with a tunnel that started near the basement, crossed Olive Street and led to downtown. Rumors about members of the James Gang hiding out in the tunnel ran rampant. As this picture below shows, Olive Street was divided by the brick wall in the foreground. The tunnel went beneath that road and wall. Heading south, a driver would have been on the high side of the road; while heading north, the driver would use the lower road. The tunnel attracted all kinds of visitors, including vagrants and children. The tunnel was finally closed off by the City of Paso Robles in 1985. The tunnel was, nearly seven feet high and led to downtown. It had a tile floor and niches in the wall (possibly for the lanterns or candles that would have provided lighting). There were many stories about the tunnel and it is a shame it was filled in, but the city was worried about lawsuits should someone get hurt or if the roof of the tunnel caved in.[30] It was reported that Mr. Robinson had three meals a day delivered to him from the Paso Robles Inn and that they used that tunnel for delivery purposes. More information about the tunnel may be found at sanluisobispo.com/news/local/news-columns-blogs/photos-from-the-vault/article39511629.html

An entire book could be written about that

---

[30] David Middlecamp. *The Tribune.* January 30, 2015.

house and tunnel and I have it on good
authority that one is in the works so I'll leave
it to the author to explore the subject in depth
(forgive the pun).

Uncle Dodo and Aunt Ruby traveled the
world. They never had children. She collected
teacups from England, plates from Bavaria.
Diamond rings from god-knows-where. They
drove a Cadillac. And he may have had
another family because every once in a while,
he would disappear. No one knew where he
went. It worried my grandmother. She might
have had a crush on him. Just sayin'. And then
he would reappear and everything would
return to normal.

The Cummings' parties were renowned;
people loved to receive invitations from the
handsome couple. Who doesn't love to party
in a beautiful home? Perhaps they were
considered avant-garde.

When Uncle Dodo died, it was not
unexpected. He had been dealt a bad blow
with bone cancer. He died at home. And when

he did, Aunt Ruby packed up a few things and closed the door to that elegant colonial look-alike and never, ever returned. She did not take a stick of furniture, a rug. Nothing. There was an ashtray with one of her husband's cigarette butts in it. The year was 1956.

She then moved in with her sisters, Great Aunt Bertha and Great Aunt Wanda, in the house at 18th and Spring Street. The house on Olive Street burned to the ground a few years later after it had been stripped of everything and vandalized. Great Aunt Bertha's son Bobby then took the Cadillac and assumed oversight of the ranch.

No will was ever found. Probate was a way of life for this early pioneer family of Paso Robles. If estates and trusts existed back then, none of the family availed themselves of them as far as I could ascertain. Why was Bertha so reckless with her property? Why did the family allow this? There are no answers to those questions. It was just a crying shame.

CHAPTER FIFTEEN:
WILLIAM ROLLO DRESSER

My grandfather was a quiet man who lived and worked on the ranch for a time. He loved the ranch and must have rolled in his grave[31] when my uncle announced that he wanted to sell the place. He loved to drive his Packard out to the ranch when I was a child to "be with it." Sunday drives were common and often grandma didn't go when I was a kid. She didn't really like the ranch.

My grandfather went by the name "Rollo" his entire life. One too many Williams,

---

[31] Grandpa's ashes were scattered out at the ranch.

perhaps. He epitomized what a Rollo should be. Being the only Rollo I have ever had the pleasure of knowing, that makes sense.

He never strayed far from home. Born in Modesto, California, in November 1888, he moved with the family to Paso Robles in 1892 and there he remained until he died on May 15, 1967.

My grandfather favored my mother and she favored him. He taught her to hunt and ride horses.

The money earned at the ranch was split among the family as they all inherited their fair share when their parents were gone. And we all know how money affects the affairs of a family. In this case, there was income and outflow. How much seed to buy? When should the beef cattle be sold? How many pounds of almonds will we shake off the trees this season? Aunt Wanda was involved in all these aspects of the family business. It was her job and she took it seriously. Of course, there would be disagreements. Bickering was a family pastime. Huffing and puffing was perfected by these siblings. With the money intertwined, it was like a daytime soap opera. I called it *As the Stomach Turns*.

And as a reminder, Great Uncle Ralph, Aunt Wanda, Great Aunt Ruby, and Great Uncle Irwin never had children. That resulted in a compressed number of family members owning a stake of the ranch (i.e., each person had a bigger share). See the family tree on page 226 for a refresher.

Ralph Dresser
26 Hillcrest Drive
Paso Robles, California 93446

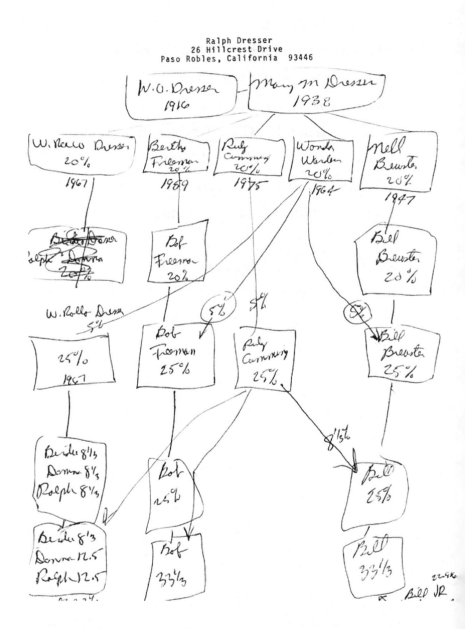

The picture included on the previous page is the only document I've found that delineates how the family inheritance was calculated. Uncle Ralph's record keeping (while not a spread sheet) was apparently effective. It depicts the Dresser family tree. It was shared with the accountant who had to follow the money for tax purposes. That was Bill Daillak and he did a remarkable job accounting for money and taxes from one generation to the next.

What's listed on the "tree" is the name and date of death of each direct descendent of the William Orlando and Mary Dresser family line from 1916 to 1975 when Great Aunt Ruby died. She was the last of my grandfather's generation. But before she died, she was in the care of a nursing home. There she developed the interesting habit of kicking people in the shins and mothering her doll. And it was because of her living situation that I discovered that she'd had a mystery mastectomy.

While dining at McPhee's restaurant in Templeton, California, a few miles south of Paso Robles one evening not too long ago, our waitress overhead me mention her name. Dian (the server) piped up and said that she knew my aunt from the nursing home, and that is how I discovered that fact. Cousin Sharon was also unaware. Further, we don't think anyone in the family outside of Dodo (Frank Cummings) knew.

Times have changed, haven't they? Mastectomies are not hidden today. Many women who've had this life-saving surgery, like our daughter-in-law, Tamara, fully acknowledge their situation. It is a much better environment now for people with cancer. With medical advances and the "shame" of cancer now relegated to history, we do live in a better world.

CHAPTER SIXTEEN:
AND THEN THERE WAS MY GRANDFATHER AND GRANDMOTHER

William Rollo and Birdie Dresser

Photo of 1 Dresser Place, credit Tim Bryan

In 1922, my grandparents married in Long Beach, California, where Old Mother (that was my grandmother's mother) lived. When grandpa and grandma returned to Paso Robles from their wedding, they lived on the ranch, which was six miles from town. Doesn't sound very far in today's world, but it might as well have been Missouri. My grandmother didn't drive, so she was stuck out there on the ranch unless she wanted to ride a horse to town. Or so I thought until I unearthed a typed "diary" that my great grandmother authored. It was entitled, *Record of "Our Garden at Lane's End House."* It reveals what daily life was on the ranch. An excerpt:

"February 27, 1937. Going into town this afternoon to see a show and get supplies. Our first show since Xmas. "Go and Get It." Finally got into town after much difficulty, having many interruptions before parting, such as, a man having to be pulled out of the river, and finally got started. On the way we saw some of Rollo's cows in the wheat and had to stop and chase them out. Well, we just arrived in time for the start of the show and it was really a

wonderful show. I had my glasses fixed, $2.00. We bot our grocerie(s) and got home via the sled-wagon. Had supper with Birdie and home about 9:00 , so went to bed, all tired out.

"February 28 Today we were invited to Birdie's for Chicken dinner. Donna, Ralph and Bill came for us & just in the middle of the river, the sled broke & the horses and the front end went on and we sat still. Well, it was funny. Off went our shoes and we waded on across, lots of laughs. Also waded back at nite. Ha ha.

"March 19 Today Birdie drove over alone & said Rollo thot we had better go to town if we wanted to, as both Dad's Government Checks came."

Evidently, early on while living at the ranch, grandma did drive. How it came to be that she stopped driving is a mystery for the ages.

While I'm unsure of exact dates, I believe they lived there from 1922 at the Samuelson place then moved to town, living on Vine Street, and returning to the ranch from 1933 until 1938. They were there during the Great Depression and I'm told that grandma cooked for a crew working at the ranch during that terrible time. She regarded herself as genteel and it must have made her wonder what the heck she had gotten herself into by marrying my grandfather. That was a feeling that was with her always.

Within a year of their marriage, she gave birth to my mother—a ten-pound baby delivered by the petite, bird-like woman strains the imagination. Birthing took place at my great grandparents' house on Spring Street. Dr. Ralph Dresser, my grandfather's brother, was the physician in attendance. It may have been awkward.

Four years later, she gave birth to Uncle Ralph. He was always the favorite child and his mother let that show.

My grandmother was a force to be reckoned with. She was a small woman, about five foot two with eyes of blue. Bette Davis eyes, I'd say. So many pictures of her in later life show her with a martyr like look on her face. Woeful, sad—like looks that would cause a person to wonder, "What the heck is on her mind, anyway?" Most of the people who knew my grandmother, thought better of her. This favorability view was not reciprocated by her in many cases because the fact of the matter was that she was quite judgmental of people and their antics. I know this because she often confided her opinions while telling one of her rambling stories.

You see, she was a stream-of-consciousness orator. The story would start out with, say, a story about a friend who went to the dentist and by the time she was finished, it involved tales about the dentist's wife, the dental

assistant's father, the property a friend of the
dentist had up there on Vine Street. The horse
that they kept in a corral behind the house.
That would then morph into the story of the
old mare busting out of the corral, the broken
fence, the man that came to fix the fence, the
neighbor that chased down the horse, the
lineage of the horse, the person that made the
horse's hoofs, and, oh, by the way, the
disposition of the bad tooth of her friend.

She was so adept at telling these stories that
her son, my Uncle Ralph, would barge into the
story by exclaiming, "Get to the end of this
story. Where is the end of the story, Mother?"
He spoke in a rather forceful manner that
betrayed his lack of interest, his lack of
etiquette, and his utter lack of patience.

She would then finish up the story without
leaving out important details, completely
aware of the dynamics and quite possibly
wondering how she spawned this rude child,
with a rather sad and dejected look upon her
face like she was just informed that her best

friend just died. In time, my Uncle's rude comments would recede into the past and another story would pop up which would start the cycle all over again. I rather enjoyed her marauding tales of things so very important to her...things that the average person would hardly take note of let alone share with family and friends alike... and it made me angry that he would show such insensitively. I mean, who was he to be rude to her? She favored him at every turn, at each eventuality, in all things at the expense of the rest of her motley crew which was her nuclear family. In a word he was insufferable. Be that as it may, Grandma Bird, oh, dear, Grandma Bird. She could tell a story.

She was neither over weight nor slender, landing right in the middle of body styles, with a good set of knockers, slim hips, bird legs and small feet. Here I take pause to say that I mention her feet as small because in comparison to my clodhoppers, they were tiny. Her feet were narrow and buying shoes required special sizes... a AAAA heel and maybe a AAA toe. She was a hard fit in the shoe department and add to the fact that she took great pains to make the decision, buying shoes was like a half day event. Being self absorbed, I don't have any earthly idea how she ever found shoes that fit her. There were no Nordstrom in Paso Robles. Or San Luis Obispo. And there was no Amazon or Zappos. Life was hard for the shoe shopper in that era. She may have ordered shoes through the L.A. Times somehow. Yes, I think she did buy shoes from the Times and she often stole good ideas for outfits from the Style section of that newspaper. It was her go-to reference for keeping up appearances like Hyacinth Bucket, the woman in that hilarious *Keeping Up Appearance* show featured on BBC.

In those days, newspapers would bring the news of the world to your doorstep. And you know what else? Sears and Montgomery Wards were also delivered to the door. Big clumps of catalogues were produced a couple of times of year and receiving your catalogue was like receiving the Pottery Barn "catalogue" on steroids. These catalogues were useful if one wanted to buy a house (yes, Sears sold houses in their catalogues), order a drill, swoon over a dress, and dream the dreams these tomes offered to people that lived in rural communities. When I discovered these catalogues, my fertile mind was beginning to show signs of life; and it was when I discovered geography mattered because when you read the price of the thing you absolutely could not live without, the price included the phrase "Prices slightly higher West of the Rockies."

Leafing through the one big giant sales pitch was fun and after people were tired of doing that or had since placed their order for the things they wanted, they put those heavy duty books to other uses such as toilet paper, wrapping paper, doorstops, bookcase filler, and occasionally, I'm guessing they may have proved useful to hurl at someone while in a rage.

But I digress.

She had a good head of thick hair and, with that well proportioned figure, she looked good draped in her handmade clothes. Sewing was one of the ways she expressed herself. Her artistry at the Singer was undeniable as she sat perched over it, pumping her feet up and down on the iron step that sat near the floor. The treadle. Besides providing the power for the machine, it strengthened leg muscles. Sewing was her forte.

The Singer sewing machine was located in the tiny kitchen, in front of the east facing window which afforded her a view of the backyard. It also allowed her to escape the heat of summer as the sun came around to the west on those hot, Paso Robles afternoons. In front of the Singer, was her kitchen table that was called into service daily for either the three meals which she dutifully prepared and served, or by rolling out cookie dough around the holidays, or rolling out a pie crust the rest of the year, or by laying out material to pin a pattern to so that the material could be transformed into a dress.

Her sewing was renowned in the family. She made my mother's clothes and my clothes. She did not do sewing for the men. That was way too boring for her. After all, what did men wear in those days? Button down shirts and trousers. And dungarees. No skill or imagination was required.

But dresses, now you are talking about something. Darts at the bosom, hems of various lengths, sleeves or not, gathers or straight. Decisions were required. This occurred once she had perused the L.A. Times fashion section. Once the pattern was selected, it was on to the bolts of material that took up the center of the room at the Mercantile, the local department store which was located across from the city park on one side, and the Paso Robles Press newspaper building on the other side. The vibrant colors, the feel of the material, the sheerness or heaviness required were considered. So many decisions for her to make. It was a healthy diversion, I am sure. It took her away to someplace else, away from the melancholy that infected her being.

In this picture, you can see her style. Jacket with pocket square sporting a handkerchief, she looks quite happy. And my Mom was so pretty in her handmade blouse which Grandma Bird made. Grandma Bird was 47 years old in this picture. My mother was 23. Old mother (a title of endearment) was 60.

My Mom, Grandma, Bird, me, and my Great Grandmother

I've got to hand it to my grandmother. With her background, she found outlets to fill the time and move forward.

Grandma Bird was born in 1898 in Kansas

City, Missouri. She arrived in San Luis Obispo with her mother, Agnes, and father, Arthur Luttrell. The oldest of many siblings that were to follow, she did not know that her father was not her biological father. That information did not present itself until my great grandmother (Old Mother)) lay dying on her deathbed.

The conversation may have been: "Your father (Luttrell) was not your father. Your father was Sherman Noble(s). He deserted me (my assumption) when I announced my pregnancy. So I met Arthur and married him and gave you his name as respectability required."

And there she had it. The unvarnished truth that must have shocked my grandmother to her core…although she may have told someone in the family that it solved the mystery as to why she always felt like the odd person out. And this goes a long way in saying that it no doubt contributed to her emotional state. This happened in the late 1940s. She was approaching 50 years of age.

Grandma Bird was a wonderful woman who signed up for a hard life. Why? My grandfather, at some point, fell in love with the bottle. He loved to drink, gamble, and play snooker. As his role as the ranch manager waned, the pool hall became his main line of work.

My grandfather, William Rollo Dresser, married my grandmother when he was thirty five. She was twenty five. I lack stories about him because he was often at the pool hall, the ranch or running errands for his sisters. He was quiet, unassuming, and often times high from drinking Seagram's Seven and puffing on Parliament cigarettes. He wore suspenders and Stetson hats. That look was finished off with hightop shoes that laced. He also enjoyed peace and quiet and I disrupted that, so sometimes he was not pleased with my activities like practicing the piano. "Stop that drumming!", he would yell when I was drumming on the upright piano in the living room.

At some point someone bought me a blue parakeet which I named Casper. Grandpa would try to befriend Casper but that bird was mean. There were a few swear words uttered when he would stick his finger through the bars of the birdcage. He should not have been doing this because he was a bleeder. Great care was taken by everyone to see that he did not cut himself.

My grandmother was always trying to get him to church. One X-mas he went to church with us and fell asleep in the pew. We knew he was asleep because of his loud snoring. Then as he was leaving the church, he lost his footing on the stairs and tumbled to the sidewalk. He never graced the church with his presence again. And grandma didn't ask him to either.

Returning to the Ranch for a Bit

Roberta Barrett, a long-time Paso Roblan, remembers the ranch well for a couple of reasons. Her mother was born at the ranch in the house at 1 Dresser Place. Her grandfather Morie Barba and her grandmother Sallie lived in the house when Morie was working at the ranch as the main ranch hand. Additionally, Barney Moraga, Sallie's brother, ran cattle out on the ranch. When Sallie gave birth in 1927, the creek was roaring and the doctor had to forge the creek using a rope in order to deliver the baby, Roberta recalled.

Some time after that was when my grandparents moved out there.

There were windmills, poison oak, rattlesnakes, and deer. Dove and quail. Wild mushrooms. It was a great place for hunters. My grandfather prided himself on his deer- and dove-hunting abilities and he passed that onto my mother, who became quite a good shot. The first day of deer season was a very big deal. Who could get their deer on the first day had bragging rights. My grandfather was very competitive in the game, getting up before dawn and out to the ranch. I heard rumors that sometimes he cheated. Cheating must have meant that he a shot deer he shouldn't have. There were rules. The rules are complicated, which that is how I found myself enrolled in Hunterman's Safety. For the record, I was no Annie Oakley. I never killed an animal... just couldn't do it.

During the '30s, my grandparents moved back to town.

When my grandparents moved out to the ranch, they lived at 1 Dresser Place. It lacked indoor plumbing. And I suppose this is why my grandmother years later, still squatted over the chamber pot she stowed under her bed rather than take about eight paces to her porcelain toilet in the bathroom. Yes, in the dead of winter. There was no insulation between sheet rock or plaster and the outer skin of their house at 1612 Oak Street and still, with the windows flung open, she would get up and adorn the chamber pot as she held up her flannel nightie. Really. You could freeze a ham in that bedroom.

But the chamber pot lived on. I know because I lived with my grandparents for a spell and she made me do the same thing. Luckily I was young and didn't have to "tinkle" too much at night. But I did it too and it made no sense. I'd say, "But grandma, the toilet is right next to this bedroom." Made no difference to her. This is the way tinkling at night took place, and she was bound and determined to keep up the habit come hell or high water (if you'll pardon the pun). I was only around ten years old so what could I do? Squat.

My grandfather, for his part, peed in a mayo jar that he kept bedside on Oak Street. His bedroom (they had separate bedrooms) was directly across the hall from that same bathroom. There were actually two doors that opened to the bathroom, one from the hall, and one from my grandma's bedroom (a very

modern concept way back then). My
grandfather, being an alcoholic who owned a
pool hall (that other career once they moved
to town), never got up in the middle of the
night since he was pretty much passed out
until morning. However, the mayo jar was
emptied into the toilet now and again.

They didn't sleep together and they didn't
use the toilet at night. Geez. As far as I knew,
perhaps everyone did this. As a young girl
with no siblings, whom could I ask? And how
would I present that question: "Do your
parents share a bed? Do they piddle in the
toilet in the middle of the night?"

In addition to the ranch, there was another
source of income for the family: the Standard
gas station. It was the parcel directly across
18th Street from Aunt Wanda's house. It was a
"filling station." On July 1, 1984 Chevron
became the owner of the gas station. Chevron
leased the land and paid the family a
handsome sum for the trouble. My grandfather
also was involved in that station and worked

there at one time. About the only story I can remember hearing about the Chevron station was that my grandfather, Rollo, hoisted a car up on the hydraulic thing that gas stations have and the car fell partially off. Was this true? I wasn't there. That was the family rumor. Or family folklore. Whenever the story was told, there was laughter involved so I assume it wasn't a horrible ending.

Doyle Rose replaced my grandfather to excellent effect at the gas station. Doyle Rose was beloved by those who knew him and he was always friendly, kind, and capable. It was a very good association.

Next door to the station was the house where my mother and uncle were born. As noted previously, it was my great-grandparents' house. The address was 1733 Spring Street. Originally I thought perhaps it was a house where women gave birth because my mom and uncle were born there. With help from the Paso Robles Area Historical Society (PRAHS), I discovered the fact that it was owned by the Dressers.

Today, it is a parking lot. The house was torn down years ago. What remains are two paintings and one photo of the house.

Because women are such important historical persons, I must introduce you to my grandmother's side of the family.

CHAPTER SEVENTEEN:
THE LUTTRELL FAMILY TIES

"Behind every great man is a woman rolling her eyes."

JIM CARREY

My grandmother, child on the right. Taken in San Luis Obispo, circa 1903 Stepfather Arthur Luttrell, and mother left. William Orlando and Mary Dresser are seated.

Grandma Birdie Luttrell obtained a teaching credential from San Jose Normal

School (aka San Jose State aka San Jose State University) and taught school on the central coast of California before she married my grandfather.

My grandmother, though married to a farmer, was not a gardener as far as I know. Living all those years on the ranch (which she loved to hate), I think it can be assumed, gardening wasn't her favorite past time. Her interests were in the area of cooking, reading, sewing, decorating, knitting. She was very good at the first three. My love of cooking is a direct hand-me-down from her. Cooking on a shoestring was her style. She took her love of reading and subscribed to the *Los Angeles Times* (as mentioned earlier), and this is where she gleaned recipes that were up-to-the-minute. She also eschewed the new Swanson's TV dinners that popped onto the scene in the 1950s.

While she had her tried-and-true recipes, she loved to try new dishes. She used to freak me out by cooking brains. And mushrooms that grandpa had forged for out at the ranch. OMG. My fear of dying was on full alert when the mushrooms were being sautéed in a pound of butter. Who was going to expire on the kitchen floor after nibbling on the fungus? Well, it was not about to be me. No way would I eat a mushroom and I held resolutely to that opinion until I was divorced and acquired an open mind on food. Not sure what the divorce had to do with it, but that is when pizza with mushrooms became something I would gobble down with great gusto.

Grandma had a habit of snipping recipes from the *Times* and then often combining her love of cooking with sewing as she pinned the recipes into a "book" of recipes she kept. Straight pins were in great abundance, so she repurposed them from sewing to saving recipes. And often she wrote notes on the recipes she cooked… she was way ahead of TripAdvisor or Yelp.

She had another claim to fame. She hiked up Morro Rock. That is no longer allowed except for Indigenous people and a few others.

en.wikipedia.org/wiki/Morro_Rock for more information.

My grandmother was an Episcopalian, and a great lover of a deal. This combination led her to be a great fan of rummage sales. She spent great time and effort to drag old things down to the church hall and donate them. Of course, in order for the church to thrive, she perused the tables of old clothes and knickknacks in search of things she could buy to haul back home. My grandfather was always amazed at this. Everything she brought back from the rummage sale had a story attached... Mrs. Petersen's lamp, Mr. Smith's cane. The stories were entertaining and informative, but they drove Uncle Ralph crazy. She would pontificate as long as someone was in the room. He always left the dinner table early, I think because of these stories.

My grandmother's step-siblings were an entirely different matter. My familiarity with them was limited. We lived in Paso Robles, and they all lived in Southern California. My grandmother's oldest sister was Great Aunt Rachel.

Nota Bene: Paso Robles was and is situated half way between Los Angeles and San Francisco near the coast. Highway 101 runs through it.

Great Aunt Rachel Luttrell Schick married Charles Schick, who was a brilliant young man with talent galore. He ended up as a movie producer in the employ of Metro-Goldwyn-Mayer, a nice little Irish company in Culver City, California. As such he hobnobbed with the stars of the time: Laughton, Pickford, and the likes. My great aunt entertained them while she wasn't practicing Mozart and Bach. As an accomplished piano and harpsichord musician, she "tickled the ivories" with the classical composers. She loved Bach and studied under a teacher that was well-know in music circles. While her playing inspired me, I did not follow in her footsteps re: the piano.

Aunt Rachel was a wonderful woman and she was unconventional. She received a degree in the 1950s by going back to school at an older age. I doubt many women in those years did that. She became a member of the AAUW organization that is comprised of colleges educated women that provide help to other women. Membership in 1960 was 147,000 plus according to Wikipedia. She was one of them.

Charles Schick was a great find for the Luttrell clan. He saw to it that all Great Auntie's siblings were gainfully employed by the studios. It's who you know, isn't it? Great Uncle Jimmy worked for Technicolor. Great Uncle Charles married Great Aunt Agnes, Grandma Bird's youngest sister by eighteen years. Great Uncle Charles was a film editor. He worked on *Dr. Zhivago* and other films. Great Uncle Jimmy was a set manager. He had his picture taken carrying Lana Turner over a mud puddle (on the one day it actually rained in L.A.). The picture made it into one of the movie magazines of the day. Jimmy married Betty, and she was a script holder for the stars. Great Uncle Edwin did something at the studios, I don't remember what. Maybe Technicolor. The unlucky sibling was Great Uncle Arthur. Gifted with a wonderful voice, he died in his twenties of throat cancer.

Recently, I came upon an old scrapbook and in it there were holiday telegrams from Heddy Lamarr, Mr. Mayer, and a few other notables that were sent to my great uncle. On the telegram, his last name was spelled "Chic." Charles Chic. It is unknown to me why his name was spelled thus. Perhaps as a Jewish person, he wanted some privacy during World War II.

Great Aunt Agnes Luttrell Ennis

Great Aunt Agnes was known for her good looks and sense of humor. She genuinely laughed at seemingly everything and appropriately so. Everyone loved her laugh. Because she wanted children rather than fame and fortune as an actress, she had four children. They were my mom's first cousins, but because they were close to my age, I felt they were like my first cousins. I loved being with them: Jimmy, Tony, Chris, and Katy. Agnes and Chuck stopped producing children once Katy, the only girl, came along. The thing was that Great Uncle Chuck, her film-editing husband had a problem with the bottle. He eventually joined Alcoholics Anonymous and was a member for fifty-five years. This caused him to be a crank, according to my cousins, who knew a thing or two about it. He was also very handy and taught his sons how to be useful around the house. Problem was, he had no patience, so learning was torturous. Chuck and Agnes stayed married until she died in the '70s. He outlived her by many years. Perhaps he was pickled early on and pickling became an act of self-preservation.

These brief descriptions don't get to some really interesting things. Except for my Grandma Bird, all her siblings were serious party animals. Smoking and drinking, drinking and smoking. As a youngster, I didn't appreciate the enormity of the situation. However, my Uncle Ralph held the parties in high esteem. He recounted to me on more than one occasion that the family would congregate in Beverly Hills at one of their homes and start the drinking. As they ran out of booze, a taxi was called, an order was placed, and another bottle would arrive, thanks to the cabbie. Everyone was invited to dinner but drinking ruled the night and if they were lucky, some food would be served, often well past 11 p.m. These gatherings were happy occasions with jokes and stories in-between sipping (slurping?) their drinks.

Nowadays, I guess you would get on your cell phone, look up the app, put in the order. These relatives may have been the first wave using this procedure to procure their libations when under the table. Today we have Grubhub and Doordash and Instacart.

Great Uncle Edwin

Great Uncle Edwin was quite the character. He fancied himself a great storyteller. And he was. It was great fun to listen to him because no one ever knew if the story was true or not. He had a gift for entertaining. When he was in school, he won an essay contest and collected a prize. It was later discovered that he plagiarized the entire essay. Not sure if the sponsors clawed the prize back or not. But this made him famous with family members and everyone always gathered around when he started talking. He could wax poetic for hours (or at least it felt like hours). The relatives in Southern California may have seen it a differently. Apparently as he told his stories, the stories would change in noticeable ways, which seemed to frustrate everyone to no end. However, distance made his musing particularly funny and entertaining to those of us living in Paso. He was married and had a daughter, Laura. Laura was pretty and smart. She graduated from USC. However, she veered away from the family so no one knows her history. She was an alcoholic with diabetes and died in 2022.

Great Uncle Jimmy

Great Uncle Jimmy married a woman named Betty. They had no children. She also worked for the studios. He traveled on his job to Tahiti for the movie, *Mutiny on the Bounty.* He had a houseboy who had a child out of wedlock that he and Betty ended up adopting. That was one of his acquisitions there. He also ran into the artist Letteg. Letteg chose to paint on black velvet. He especially loved to paint nude women. Jimmy ended up with one of his paintings. No one seemed to know anything about the artist Letteg. Then one weekend when I was down visiting Grandma Bird, we were watching a program on TV and up pops Letteg's name. At that very same time, grandma had repurposed the painting which was unframed and lived in the linen closet … repurposed it to be a drop cloth for an old wash bowl and pitcher in her bedroom (which was being painted at the time). So, I rushed back to the bedroom to see if it was an original or not. YES. She had an original and she didn't like it all. So, I took it, had it "cleaned up and framed" and took it to San Francisco for an appraisal. It was maybe worth $15,000. This was about 1967. Once she considered the value, she decided she liked it after all and took it away from me. Oh, well, where does one hang a picture of nude native woman, with a red-and-white sarong across her lap as she posed with both hands behind her head? Grandma Bird kept that painting until she died. And she never hung it up anywhere. It lived behind a piece of furniture.

The Third Generation

"The secret of a happy marriage remains a secret."

HENNY YOUNGMAN

CHAPTER EIGHTEEN:
DRIVING AND EAR DRUMS
AND OTHER STORIES

I think it can safely be said that my
grandfather was a glutton for food and drink.
At one point in his life as recently reported, he
weighed 300 pounds. This must be the reason

that there existed in their bathroom with
funny wallpaper a bath tub as big as state of
Texas. It was extra long and deep. At 300
pounds, he looked like Winston Churchill.
Grandma Bird snipped a picture of Sir
Winston out of *Life* magazine, framed it, and
hung it over the sofa in the living room. Sir
Winston wore a sash across his chest and on his
lapel were all his medals he had earned,
probably in the course of WWII. Friends
would come by to visit, notice the picture and
exclaim, "Oh, Birdie, Rollo looks so good in
that picture. Where on earth did he get all
those medals?"

Actually, Winston was the recipient of many
medals from many various campaigns. And he
was the recipient of a Nobel Prize but it was
not for his leadership during WWll. It was a
prize for literature.

Because of time out at the ranch, my
grandmother was very parsimonious with
water. She used a tiny portion of the great big
tub in the Oak street house. Her idea of

bathing was to draw a thimble full of water, squat by the tub's water faucet and throw water on herself. Then she would soap up a wash cloth, wash herself, drain the water (that took a good two seconds), and turn on the cold water, splash herself as if taking a final rinse, and call it a bath. She was an original environmentalist. She saved water like it was gold. And this can be easily explained because she lived in quasi desert of California. Rain was the subject de jour every day at the kitchen table. "When do you think it will rain?" "Rain is in the forecast." And as part of a mostly dry-farming family of ranchers, rain was everything. Didn't rain, no grain. Didn't rain, no barley. Want a bath? Don't use too much water.

My grandfather, by the time I came to live with them, had lost most of his weight and suffered from gout. He ate everything and drank Seagrams Seven and Four Roses. Actually, he probably drank everything else too. I mention Seagram's and Four Roses

because when he left this world, the garage
was cleaned out and about 500 empty bottles
were found "hidden" in the garage. There were
even bottles in the tank of the toilet. The
garage was detached from the house. In the
garage were two basins, an unused Maytag
washer, and a toilet. When he went out to
garage to relieve himself, it gave him the time
and place to continue his alcoholism in peace.
Without prying eyes. Everyone knew he was
doing this. But that was the charade and it
went on for years.

Grandma Bird could be bold when sewing,
cooking, reading. What she wasn't bold about
was driving a car.

In the alley directly across the alley from
grandma's unattached garage, a huge oak grew.
And next to the south wall of the garage was a
big steel pole that had been installed by the
Jordans to help support the huge TV antenna
they had installed. Jeepers, creepers. It was
mighty tall and it could be rotated by a gizmo
that sat on top of the TV set in their house. As

the antenna searched for signals by actually rotating, it made a loud clicking sound. It rivaled KPRL's antenna (the local radio station), for heaven's sake. It was not long after the cable hardware for the antenna had been installed when my grandma decided to take driving lessons from Mr. Asa, the teacher at the high school.

Mr. Asa came to the house and they got in the car in the garage, and my grandmother put the Plymouth Valiant in reverse, hit the gas pedal, went sailing across the alley, and hit that big oak tree. Then she put it into drive by pushing a button, stepped on the throttle, and plowed right into the big pole that held the guide wire to the antenna. We family folks howled about that for years. She never made it out of the alley.

The only other time she got in the car with Mr. Asa, she ran the car directly into a big bush. That resulted in her never, ever attempting to drive again. I'm quite sure Mr. Asa was relieved. She was what is now referred to as hopeless. Nervous as a whore in church. She just couldn't do it.

Her reason for taking those lessons? Early one morning I was sitting with grandma in the kitchen probably waiting for breakfast. Grandpa entered.

"I can't hear."

And there began a new chapter in the lives of all of us. Grandpa, it seems, when he was young man, burst an eardrum. Don't know how. Just know what I was told. I could imagine it might have involved a gun. A loud explosion. So that was one ear that was out of commission. This particular morning so long ago happened while in a quiet house. Apparently it was caused by a blood clot that dried up in his ear canal. He could walk, he could talk, but he could not hear.

Flummoxed is what we were. Now what? Sign language was really out of the question. Too old or perhaps a shortage of sign language teachers? I'm not sure what was decided or not decided but my grandparents went on with life with my grandfather talking loud and grandmother writing. She had good enough penmanship so he could read her notes to him. And often she would read the words out loud as she wrote them down. It was something to behold. When they argued, her handwriting would get bigger and the lead got darker. And she would talk louder—as if that would help.

"ROLLO, I TOLD YOU TO QUIT PUTTING THE ASHTRAY DOWN LIKE THAT..."

"ROLLO, I CAN'T GO ON LIKE THIS..."

These screeds on paper could be found all over the house but mostly on the kitchen table. And of course, he would yell back and answer and she would yell back a statement and the writing would get ever bigger.

"I'M NOT GOING TO DO THAT. NO. NO. NO."

Ags 24/53

"Prais God from whome all Blessings flow"

My Dear Sarah

Last evening about eleven o'clk I anared from the Ocean steamer "Northern light" upon Tera firma to me Tera incognito, vulgarily caled New York, after as favourable a journey as man could with or heart desire; & very short at that a few hours over twenty two days I am, thank God, in good health, the passengers enjoyed remarkable good health, and to crown my good feelings I was made to rejoyce in reading a letter from your own Sign manuel, which it self was enough to gratify a weary heart, yourself better & the child and the rest well, Again I say Prais G—d I have seen nothing of the city yet for the first theing this morning was to go to the Post Off the next to comply with your request in writing you the good news that I am on this side of land, what inducements I shall find to cause me to stay I know not but don't look very hard until some time next week, recolect this is my made visit to any considerable city and this too a a very extraordenary ocasion

I put up at the New haven house corner of Broadway & Canal St a very respectable house but not extravegantly dear, tel the children when they see something come whizzen that will be Pa

Your ever loveing Husband

Sarah Dresser

Wm Dresser

Their lives became instantly harder. Grandpa couldn't work, leaving him stuck at home. He couldn't drive. His license was revoked. Because grandpa really missed driving, he took it upon himself to go out to the garage and sit in the Plymouth Valiant, start the Valiant, and proceed to race the engine. He couldn't hear it, but he could feel it vibrate and that was enough for him. By this time he had run out of booze in the garage so revving the engine replaced drinking in the garage.

Having run low on Four Roses, he decided he liked wine. So, whenever he could, he would have me drive him to the wineries. In the 1960s, there was Pesenti (now Turley), Rotta, and York (now Epoch) wineries. These were predated by the Friar monks vineyards, which were planted as the monks established missions throughout California. And as luck would have it, there were missions in San Miguel and San Luis Obispo and San Antonio. But in the sixties, the only wineries around that I knew about were Pesenti, Rotta, and York. It was Pesenti that my grandfather liked to visit. I would drive him there (no age restrictions for me to go inside the winery) where he would perch on an upside down half wine barrel, and drink what was offered. I remember big jugs of wine. The wine was poured into mason jars, or water glasses. No fine stemmed fancy glasses there. No, the first tasting rooms in the Paso Robles region were barebones, no-frills affairs without tables, chairs, bars, or anything. And no tasting fees. Invariably, grandpa would buy a couple of jugs and we'd lug the jugs back home. Then he and grandma would have their "drinking discussion."

"Wine is good for you. You should drink some," he would proclaim.

"Oh, you old fool. You bought that for yourself. Shame on you," she would scribble on the closest piece of paper.

And away they would go. Another day, another dust-up.

CHAPTER NINETEEN:
DOWN IN THE MUD
AND OTHER TIDBITS

One night, when it was raining cats and dogs, he did not arrive home for dinner. This was unusual. Far be it from him to miss a good meal. Anyway, a search ensued, and he was found out in the back alley of the pool hall, laying in the mud and battered by rain. He couldn't get up. I think Bobby Freeman went down and found him and somehow got him up, into the car, and deposited at home. This without the use of a crane. Fairly impressive. My grandmother was mad as a wet hen.

On "regular" nights, he would come home from the pool hall and have dinner. Then he would move himself to the couch in the living room, drape one leg up on the back of the couch and fall dead asleep while grandma and I would settle in for rousing evening of listening to *Gildersleeves*, the radio program. And *Amos and Andy*. And *The Shadow*. Grandma would brew tea, guaranteeing that she would have a fitful night of sleep, and then sit by the radio knitting. Or hemming a dress or something. She was always doing something. Grandpa, for his part, fell dead asleep and snored and sputtered while lying on his back with his right leg draped over the back of the couch like an old saddle might be thrown over a fence. Then when the programs were done, grandma would roust grandpa and implore him to go to bed. Which he did. And he would, again, fall fast asleep... no apnea there.

The next morning he would arise and have his daily breakfast of eggs basted in bacon fat, bacon, toast slathered with butter, and coffee. And off he'd go to the pool hall after discussing the weather with Mrs. Schmuck (pre-hearing loss). Yep. That's what he would call grandma when... well, I don't know when. All I know is that he often called her Mrs. Schmuck. She did not like him to call her Mrs. Schmuck.

Before the Valiant, grandpa drove a Packard, which I remember as very big and lumbering. Sitting in the back seat, I couldn't see out the window very well so I had no idea where he was stopping to let me out of the car to puke from being car sick. The road running from Paso Robles to Atascadero to Morro Bay to Cayucos involved too many twists and turns for this child. I'm quite sure that the Packard may have been his first car after the horse and buggy because when he stepped on the brake of the Packard, he would always say, "Whoa!"

Paso Robles was a rural town. Guns were kept in the closets in the bedrooms, except my grandmother's closet. That Bird didn't hunt. There were no guns in her closet. Now guns need to be under lock and key. It wasn't that way then. They were just leaned up against the inside wall of the closet, two or three in every closet. It was no big thing. But we didn't have mass shootings at schools either. The mental institutions were still in business. Actually, Atascadero State Hospital, located 11 miles from Paso Robles, opened in 1954 so it existed during this time. We were more concerned about the A-bomb than we were about guns. Guns were for bird hunting, deer hunting and squirrel hunting. That was it. Oh, how this country has stumbled.

Grandpa used to clean his guns in the backyard. He stored his ammunition in his dresser drawer along with spare change, garters, and suspenders. And something that held in his hernia.

I never, ever saw my grandmother and grandfather show real affection toward one another. Saying, "I love you," was not a thing in any house I ever lived in as a child or young adult. Their relationship by the time I entered the scene was one of tit for tat. My grandmother hated that my grandfather drank. My grandfather loved to drink and those two facts never got reconciled. She tried everything to get him to stop. Beaking like a bird. Barking like a dog. Pouting like a woman betrayed. Over the years she developed the art of the martyr to great effect. But who could blame her? There she was, stuck with two kids,

320 | From Beloit to Clark Gable

and she did not work outside the home after marriage. Her life was a microcosm of so many women during that era. They were just stuck, like the coal miners Tennessee Ernie Ford sang in his hit song, "16 Tons."

At one point she asked my uncle if she should just leave grandpa (his father). That was a crucial mistake because when he said no, she was not just stuck, she was trapped. There was no going anywhere. Uncle Ralph was her pride and joy and he could do no wrong. By asking him, she probably knew deep down that she would abide by his opinion. And she did. He said no. And so she stayed. Asked later when she was lying in a nursing home, barely able to swallow for several years, she said her big regret was staying with Grandpa. Interestingly too, she had given up on God. She had been a loyal member of the Episcopal church, but abandoned it in the end. In the '60s she bought new carpet for the church. She dutifully donated. She saw to it that I followed in her footsteps regarding attending church and participating in the church (until I became agnostic and then atheist). My mom and uncle—neither of whom had any interest in the church themselves—arranged for the front stained-glass window of the church to be donated with grandma's name inscribed at the bottom. They thought she would approve of the stained-glass memorial. I'm not so sure.

My grandfather had several hobbies other than sneaking out for a drink. He played cards, he watched the Gillette *Friday Night Fights*, he hunted dove, quail, and deer, and he foraged for mushrooms.

About those cards. He was quite the poker player and when traveling card sharks came to the area, he would get a call to play. Not only did he play. He won. And it might take all night but he would usually prevail. One of the tales of the times was when he traveled to Morro Bay to play at Happy Jacks, a local saloon (now The Siren). He did stay all night at the table and came home with wads of cash. The pots were big. He loved the thrill of the game.

As he aged, his card playing changed to organized card games with three other men. They took turns hosting the games in their homes. When it was his turn to host, grandma made fancy shrimp sandwiches with crustless bread ... very genteel of her to cut off the crusts. Doc Sobey was one of the players. (It was Doc Sobey who delivered me into this world.) I don't remember the other card players. These big men sat around a standard card table and it reminded me of *Alice in Wonderland* where the furniture was too small. In those days things were less fancy, down-to-earth even compared to now. While they played, grandma and I huddled in the kitchen. We weren't allowed near the men. She didn't seem to mind. I didn't either.

As mentioned previously, the *Friday Night Fights* were a more private affair. After dinner, he would move a chair directly in front of the TV (TVs were very small) for a better view and then he would proceed to fight the fight along with the raging bulls on TV. He would punch the air, throw a right jab, whoop and grunt. This was done both before and after he lost his hearing. About the only thing he didn't do was to get up and prance around the living room... everything was orchestrated from his chair. My sense is he did not like technical knockouts. He wanted the full fifteen rounds. The more punching, the better.

As a matter of fact, I lived with my grandparents for approximately three years. My grandfather died in 1967. His ashes were scattered out at the ranch. My grandmother is buried near her sister, Rachel Schick, in the Cayucos cemetery.

The Fourth Generation

So, I go with my uncle to his cardiologist appointment today. The nurse asks about the pills he takes. He said, "lexaprodibene." She says, "What's your strength?" He said, "Good."

DIANNA JACKSON

My mother, 'Donna Dresser, married my father, David L. Thomas during WWII. She met my dad at Camp Roberts, an Army base located 12 miles north of Paso, where she worked as a secretary. In a nutshell, my mom was attracted to men who drank. Every man she married loved to imbibe. Within two years of marriage, she divorced my dad, who loved his beer and his golf game.

My father's family moved from Cordyn, Iowa to Southern California when he was a lad. When World War II broke out, he joined the Army and was, for a time, stationed at Camp Roberts. Unfortunately my time with him was limited, chaotic, and traumatic. He was an absent father for most of my life.

Soon after the ink dried on their divorce settlement, my mother married a man named Westy Petraeus. They lived in Atascadero. That marriage was short lived. Her third marriage was to my brother's dad. They married in Las Vegas, Nevada, after a quickie divorce was obtained from Westy. She then married John Nelson. My brother was named John Nelson, Jr. Shortly after the ink dried on the birth certificate, John Nelson abandoned my mom and brother in Las Vegas. Mother and son had to get back to Paso on a Greyhound bus.

I had been left with friends in Atascadero, the Barba family. I became a ward of the court and so my grandparents rescued me. I lived with them until my mother returned. Mom,

my brother, and I slept in Uncle Ralph's
bedroom since he had left home by this time.

Speaking of Uncle Ralph, the other nut on
the nut tree was my uncle. I called him Uncle
Ralph and so did everyone else who knew me.
He was four years younger than my mother,
which meant that grandma took another baby
out to the ranch to rear (as mentioned earlier).
Uncle Ralph was the apple of my
grandmother's eye. Except that she was an
FDR fan and Uncle Ralph got hold of a book
by the economist Milton Friedman and was
thereby warped forever. He and grandma
would argue. He and Great Aunt Rachel would
argue. Politics was a big point of conversation
in the family. The disagreements persisted,
with no opinions changing. As a child, I
remember my grandmother watching the
Democratic and Republican National
conventions on television. Adlai Stevenson
was the standard bearer against Ike. He didn't
stand a chance against the famous General.
Grandma admired Adlai's intelligence. She saw

him as an intellectual and she fancied herself
an intellectual because she was a duly
appointed member of the Paso Robles Library
Board and a graduate of San Jose Normal
School (then a teacher's college. It later
became San Jose State College, and is now
referred to as San Jose State University, as
previously mentioned). Uncle Ralph liked Ike.

Uncle Ralph was an introvert with a
superiority complex. He thought he was better
and smarter than most people, which I now
find remarkable given all the stupid things he
did in his life. But there you have it. Uncle
Ralph was very good looking. Tallish, slender,
light hair, blue eyes. He never married and had
no children. That was just the way he wanted
it, apparently. Many people in town thought
he was a dandy. He was not. He had women
friends. One in particular. Shirley. He traveled
the world with her. She was his secret
girlfriend.

My mother and grandma were always
whispering about his women. They suspected

he had a lady friend but lacked the nerve to
ask him. At some level, they were afraid to
look under that rock. Mom didn't want to rock
the boat because she relied on her brother to
help her once their parents departed this
world. And grandma? I don't know why she
shied away from the topic. Perhaps it was more
fun to speculate than to know.

As an appraiser for the State Board of
Equalization in California, Uncle Ralph spent
most of his career driving around the state
appraising stuff like Disneyland. Living in
motel rooms. Eating alone. Home was Paso
Robles. He would swoop into town and my
grandmother would switch into high gear to
please him. He would bring his laundry. She
would wash it, dry it, starch it, iron it. He
would tell her what he wanted to eat. She
would cook it. He still had use of his bedroom
(which we used when he wasn't there).

About his bedroom. He had meticulously
cut out Vargas Girl pictures and hung them all
over the walls of his bedroom. Are you familiar

with the Vargas Pin-up Girls? You can google
"Vargas Girls" and take a look. As previously
mentioned, when my uncle was traipsing
around California, I slept in his room. I can
remember lying in bed and gazing up at all
those vixens. So captivated by these pictures, I
took many of them down and brought them to
my fifth-grade classroom to use for Show and
Tell. Not sure if my grandmother was more
furious or embarrassed. She came off as a
prude, so this must have been highly
embarrassing to her. But maybe all the adults
got a big kick out of it and they just didn't tell
me.

"Dianna, where did you get these?" my
teacher implored. "Oh, off the bedroom wall at
my grandma's house," I confessed. Teachers
are wonderful, aren't they? They have a lot in
common with hairdressers. They hear a part of
every story and probably spend enjoyable time
filling in the blanks as they would either like
them to be, or wish they weren't.

But wait. There was another time I got in

trouble for my intellect and highly developed sense of humor. In the fifth or sixth grade we studied South America. Each student had to fill out a map with pertinent information such as a country's main products, flora and fauna, points of interest including the capital. It was a big project. And fun. And informative. And to top it off, we were each assigned a country to report on in the presence of our parents and fellow classmates. I was assigned Peru. So after reading about Peru in the encyclopedia, I chose to report on the lakes of Peru. Specifically, Lake Titicaca and Lake Poopo. Well, that caused a stir! All the adults tittered while my classmates laughed out loud. Oh, those were the days.

But I digress.

Uncle Ralph would come back to Paso and then disappear in the evening. He went drinking at Busi's. Busi was his best friend and business partner. Busi was another confirmed bachelor (until he got married later in life). His family owned an Italian restaurant across from the city park and it was successful for years, providing Busi the bar to lord over. Busi knew everyone and everyone's business. He ruled over the most important watering hole in Paso during that time. I only remember Busi behind the bar. Not sure I saw him many other places. The bar was smallish, cozy, with a tobacco-stained bar that was an antique. Very handsome piece of furniture. Busi had a rip-roaring laugh and seeing as how Uncle Ralph had a good sense of humor, it's easy to understand why they held together their entire lives. Uncle Ralph was quite a prankster as a young man. One time he and some friends turned the lights out at the circuit breaker of a local church. He described it as a "holy roller" church, and they waited until the rolling really got going and then killed the lights. That was one of his favorite stories to tell. Busi may have been involved. I don't know.

Busi and Uncle Ralph, however, were involved in buying some land and then donating heavily to the election campaign of

Vernon Sturgeon, a state representative. That was a good move; somehow the State of California built a road right through that parcel, which connected Highway 101 to Highway 46 (west), which went up over the mountains and ended up at Highway 1 which led north to Hearst Castle. That same road today leads to wineries galore. Paso Robles is rivaling Napa Valley as a wine destination. The road is also becoming a major route for people that live in and/or visit Cambria.

It should be noted that Uncle Ralph got paid by the government he loved to hate. Actually, he was in the military twice (all Stateside), and he worked for the State of California. But he hated taxes. He didn't like government. Milton Friedman saw to that. And yet, there it was. Cognitive dissonance, served on a silver platter.

And he loved bicycling, so when he retired, he bought a Peugeot and started riding from Paso to Cayucos. That is a bicycle route that is approximately 20 miles in distance encompassing an elevation change of 2,000 feet if one utilizes Old Creek Road, a popular shortcut. It took a bit of time to get to that level of riding but he did it. Back and forth he would pedal up Highway 46 to Old Creek Road (two miles each way) and back again after a few days' stay at the home he'd purchased there. The hill was steep and the bike lane was almost non-existent. He was a legend in the area. Until age eighty-five, he rode his bike almost daily from his house high on the hill of Cayucos to Whale Rock Dam. Dressed in sweat pants with rubber bands around his ankles and a puffy orange Pillsbury Doughboy-type coat, he took to the road.

At age eight-five he discovered he had heart issues. He stopped riding as much. Three years later he shot himself behind his house on the hill in Cayucos. There is a lot more to that story, but I will leave it there. His ashes were scattered at sea.

My mom married a fourth time and stayed married until her husband, Frank Helt, died in

San Diego. She then moved to Cayucos to be
closer to the family. She died in 2003 of
pancreatic cancer. She is buried in the family
plot in Paso Robles.

Donna Dresser circa 1935

Doves are very small birds. My memory of
the doves was that grandpa would bring them
back to the house and sit in the backyard
hunched over the garbage can, plucking
feathers. Small feathers. Not sure who cleaned
them but the dove appeared on our plates for
dinner. Complete with buckshot. The adults

dug in. Not this kid. Didn't appeal to me.

Mostly it was doves. I don't recall quail, but I know there were quail dinners. And as mentioned earlier, mushrooms were also a menu item at the ranch. Oh, and Bambi. Venison was cooked during deer season. Choking it down, I swore never to eat venison again. It didn't suit me. Too gamey. My mother was a very good dove hunter as well as deer hunter. She learned to hunt while living at the ranch. And those doves explain the connection to Clark Gable.

The story goes something like this.

In 1936 my Great Aunt Rachel's husband, Charles Schick, the MGM producer, arranged for Clark Gable to go hunting at the Dresser ranch. I provide here the telegram that was sent alerting the family to Mr. Gable's impending arrival in Paso Robles. He drove into town in a fancy car with the top down. He certainly knew how to preen. The car was a

Duesenberg.

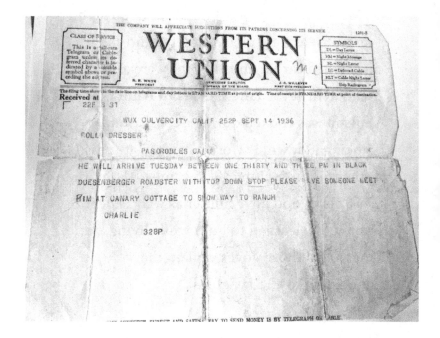

My mother in 1936 was thirteen years old. My grandmother was thirty-eight. Clark Gable was just thirty-five years old. It must have been a fabulous visit. My mother recounted it in a letter:

"One of the highlights of growing up and living on the ranch was when our

parents had as their guest, in September of 1936, Clark Gable. He arrived one afternoon for an afternoon dove hunt and another dove hunt the next morning. He stayed overnight with us and our mother cooked him a dove dinner with all the trimmings.

"Our mother was reading Gone With the Wind, and Mr. Gable mentioned he was reading it for the second time. Mother then told him if the time would come when it was made into a moving picture, he would be perfect for the part of Rhett Butler. His reply was, 'I have already thought of that!' It became a reality."

At any rate, Clark showing up with his top down… that would have been quite the sight. The car looked pretty good too, I'm guessing.

The average car cost $500 at the time. Duesenbergs could put you back about $20,000 in those days for their top-of-the-line model. In today's dollars, $20,000 would be $444,500.

Clark Gable gave my mother a signed picture of himself; the original is in the Paso Robles Historical Society building today. You can barely make out part of the inscription since it has faded over time. I wonder how I would react if, say, George Clooney came to my house for dinner. Oh my.

My mom wrote a poem to commemorate the occasion.

The Country

I.

I live on a ranch
Lots of kids don't have that chance
We have lots of sand
Besides fertile land

II.

Cattle roam the hills
And I have lots of thrills
There are horses too
And the sky is always blue

III.

A winding river flows through
To the broad Pacific so blue
The trees are very thick
It's fun to be a country hick.

IV.

The hunting is fine
I play dog part time
I did for Clark Gable
And that's no fable

V.

In the spring the birds tweet
And all the flowers smell sweet
The stock grows fat
That means ma can buy a hat.

This poem was obviously written by a young girl but it does give an idea of what life was like living on the ranch while her parents entertained a famous movie star.

And there you have it.

CHAPTER TWENTY ONE:
SALE OF THE RANCH

The Thimm Family

Mr. Thimm was the last ranch hand at the Dresser ranch. He and his wife, Marge, and their daughter, Joan, lived in the house that my grandparents had lived in during the 1930s (1 Dresser Place). The house having been constructed in 1914 had then, and still has an earthen foundation, no insulation, no double paned windows. But it came with the job, and there you are.

The Thimms had just one child. After her parents died, she and her family lived just above that old house after having previously lived in such interesting places as Bakersfield, Katy, Texas, burbs of Houston, and Angola. Yes, that Angola in Africa. In 2022, Joan and her husband sold the property which included a new, modern home that they designed and moved to Texas.

Mrs. Thimm grew up in the Willow Creek

area of Paso Robles Mr. Thimm grew up in
Nebraska. They met in Paso Robles. Daughter
Joan recalls that they moved into the house at
1 Dresser Place in September of 1958 and
lived there until 2008 after both her parents
had died. There it sat until 2006 when a niece
and her family moved in to occupy the place so
people would stop pilfering from the
yard…lots of important junk in that yard
including my grandfather's old Packard. When
the old car died a natural enough death, it was
assigned a spot in the yard, above the house.

Uncle Ralph decided that the Thimm family
should have the house and the land
surrounding the house when it came to to
selling the ranch. Perhaps he thought it a
fitting retirement present.

There was one family member, Bobby
Freeman, who would not agree to such an
arrangement. He refused to agree and further
decided that he would not sell his portion of
the acreage and house to my Uncle Ralph
when my uncle offered to buy Bobby's share of

the property. That's when shenanigans were embarked upon, and a Thimm relative that Bobby didn't know, took possession by purchasing his share. The Thimm family worked out the details and the other Dressers sold the rest of the land/house to the Thimms for $1.00.

One of the lots included in the transfer was sold to Randy Stinchfield and it is contiguous to Joan's house.

Joan had a good childhood out at the ranch. Born in 1952 and being an only child out there must have been much like my mom and uncle's experience. Joan lived there until she went away to college.

When she was about 6 years old, her father would put her into the snub nosed grain truck, where she would sit on her knees in order to see the road and reach the steering wheel, and drive the truck down the hill near the house. Mr. Thimm told her to just turn it off if she got in trouble because it would not stop for lack of breaks. Far cry from today where you have to buckle your kids into contraptions in the backseat that requires agility, patience, and pleadings. Matriculating from the kid seat to the seatbelt takes years depending, I guess, on where you live. The obvious point here is that it's amazing how pampered the children of today are compared with days gone by. Not a judgment, just an observation.

Joan lived on the ranch when the old brick house burned but she doesn't remember the actual fire. As she told me, "I used to go into that house but I wasn't allowed up the stairs. It was unsafe. But really, so was the first floor."

She also remembers the artisan well that was discovered when the family drilled for oil. That well has now dried up because of all the water that has been drawn down for homes and agriculture. The ranch was not irrigated much in earlier days. Dry farming was a much better idea than what is happening now. That's progress. Too bad.

Joan tickled me with her story about the Tulley cow. It belonged to the Tulleys and would jump any fence, anywhere to get where she wanted to go. She would jump the fence into the barnyard by the house and so she would need to be returned. Once returned, she would jump the fence where she lived, saunter over to the Thimm's and jump that fence to get in. She was a character of a cow. Other than the famous nursery rhyme about the cow jumping over the moon, I had no idea cows actually jumped anything. But the Tulley cow did.

Joan and I met up at Sculpterra Winery which sits right next to the old Dresser ranch land. As we were ambling down memory lane, I recalled that I have a picture of myself in their front yard with a baby deer which I described as a doe.

"Oh, no, that was not a doe.", she corrected me. "That was a fawn and that fawn lived with us as a pet for three years." Apparently, Mr. Thimm rescued the fawn as a baby and fed it and gave it a home. The fact that it hung around for three years astounded me. Joan reported that it never grew very big and it had nubs for antlers. But it lived around the property for all that time. That speaks to the gentle nature of the Thimms. They were fine people. The deer's name was, of course, Bucky.

When I asked Joan if she was lonely as an only child living at the ranch, she said no, she didn't. "After all, I had 10 cousins (all from the same mother) whom lived in Paso Robles, the Scantlins." Well, now, that would be fun with so many cousins to romp with.

With the Thimm gift arranged, Uncle Ralph completed the sale of the ranch. He wanted the money. He and Mom got their share of the proceeds. The sale of all the parcels on the ranch was pretty much history in 1972. From 1882 to 1972, 3,000 acres remained in the family. Other than one parcel, no one from this branch of the Dresser family now owns any land anymore. All it took was four generations... or perhaps it was amazing that it lasted that long. With characters who had competing interests, it may have been a miracle that it stayed in one family for so long.

Bob Freeman did not want to sell but all the other family members favored the idea. Bob was outnumbered. Because the land had been subdivided early on, the ranch was sold off in parcels from 5 acres to 20 acres or more. Today it has "ranchettes". People that live there love it, I've been told.

Final Thoughts

My family has quite an interesting history, which I have dutifully attempted to convey in these pages. Of course, the family is still around; I am part of the fifth generation as is my brother, John Nelson.

Looking back and researching the history has been very gratifying and I must confess that this book took a very long time to write because I was a neophyte when I started this project. This book would not have been possible without the help of a multitude of great people; I hope you take the time to read the acknowledgements.

This branch of the Dresser family is almost at an end. We saw the arrival in California of William Henry Dresser. After his wife, Sarah, died in Wisconsin, he returned to California with their children, which included William Orlando Dresser. And the roots in California grew. Being a native Californian and a

descendent of William Henry and Sarah
Dresser; a descendent of William Orlando and
Mary Dresser; and the granddaughter of
William Rollo and Birdie Dresser, I am both
amazed and in awe of what the family did
between 1847 and the 1970s (when the ranch
was sold off in parcels).

After the ranch was sold, my mother and
uncle received a nice retirement to enjoy.
Uncle Ralph spent his retirement in Cayucos,
overlooking the Pacific Ocean. He had a house
built on thirty-seven prime acres on the top of
a ridge at the ranch and then sold it because he
didn't like living there. My mom who by that
time had moved to San Jose, California, had a
boyfriend and she bought him two
laundromats so he could be gainfully
employed. Then she received a call one day
from an old acquaintance who used to hunt at
the ranch with Billy Brewster. That call ended
up with her moving to San Diego and
eventually getting married to Frank Helt, her
fourth and final husband (and another man

who just could not stop drinking).

My brother (who is now sixty nine years old) had two children. Only one of his two sons survives. I had two children, and only one of my sons survives. Neither one of our surviving sons have procreated.

The Freemans are the only branch that still carries the Dresser genes for that branch of the family.

So in a sense, as this book comes to a close, so do many limbs of the tree. Of course, other limbs have flourished and for that we are grateful.

I would like to think that this book will outlive my generation. It is an accounting of the discovery and settlement of the West. Hundreds of thousands of families have similar stories, but each with a unique experience of moving west. The Native Americans suffered through all of it. It is my hope that people interested in the history of this beautiful, wild land will expand their reading to include historic accounts of the

Native Americans. We all owe the Native Americans our respect and understanding. They suffered genocide at the hands of U.S. government. And it is not lost on me that the ranch property my family owned belonged to the Mexicans and Native Americans before it belonged to the Dressers.

Bibliography

Bagley, Will, *With Golden Visions Bright Before Them: Trails to the Mining West, 1849-1852*, p. Cm. (Overland West: The Story of the Oregon and California Trails and the creation of the mining West): University of Oklahoma, 2012

Bruff, J.D. *Gold Rush: The Journals, Drawings, and Other Papers of J. Goldsborough Bruff, Captain, Washington City and California Mining Association, April 2, 1849 - July 20, 1851. 2 vols.* Edited by Georgia Willis Read and Ruth Gaines,. New York: Columbia University Press, 1944.

Decottignies, Becky, The Dresser Letters, LoloPress.

Dresser, William. *Letters, 1850 Dresser Family Papers* MSS 69/115, Bancroft Library.

Dresser, Sarah Jenks. *Letters, 1847 -1853,* Bancroft Library.

Dobson, Mason, H. Et.al *The Book of Beloit,* The Daily News Publishing Company, January 1, 1936.

Levy, Jo Ann. *They Saw the Elephant, Women in the California Gold Rush,* Hamden, Conn. Archon Books, 1990

Morrison, Annie L. *History of San Luis Obispo and Environs, California: With Biographical Sketches of Leading men and Women of the County and Environs Who Have Been Identified With the Growth and Development of the Section from the Early Days to the Present,* Historic Record Company, Los Angeles, California, 1917.

Reid, Bernard J. *Overland to California with the Pioneer Line: The Gold Rush Diary.* Edited by Mary McDougall Gordon. Stanford, California, Stanford University Press, 1985.

Shugars, Florence Lovejoy, *The Story of Roscoe* (Baldly Printing).

Tucker, Clifford W., *Paso Robles, California 1930 - 1950: When Highway 101 Ran Through My Hometown:* History4All, Inc. 2010.

Unruh, John D., Jr., *The Plains Across and the Overland Emigrants and the Trans Mississippi West, 1840 - 1860,* Urbana: University of Illinois Press, 1979

Acknowledgments

This book was written with the help of so many people that I hardly know where to start. If you have ever written non-fiction, you will know what I mean. In fiction, the author can imagine a story and develop characters and situations. In non-fiction, you must hunt for the information, find information, provide references. What you write needs to be correct and true. Conspiracy theories are not allowed.

The book must be written after research is completed or as research is completed. Books must be read. Google must be used. In this endeavor I was blessed with old letters written by my great-great-grandparents which were archived at Bancroft Library. This was the genesis of this book. I also had letters written by great grandparents and other relatives. So thanks be to them. Thanks also to all my Dresser and Luttrell family members. They gave me the material. The material was so rich

in history, humor, and angst that there is no
way I can thank them enough. Plus most have
passed on.

My dear friends Nancy Cleland, Mary Kay
Bornfleth and Tim Bryan assisted in their own
distinct and helpful ways. Nancy read and
reread my work and helped edit the book all
along the way and Mary Kay also lent her
proofreading prowess. In addition, she
provided care for Beau, our Labradoodle, and
a place to stay now and again. Eileen Shibley
turned me on to Ben Lawless who formatted
the book and selected the cover. Tim provided
property information and he introduced me to
Dresser Winery and there I met Kory and
Catherine Burke who encouraged my endeavor
and furnished us with delicious wine to drink
as I pondered. Roberta Barrett had great
stories to share as did Joan Thimm Tyner and I
appreciate so much their input.

Jan Cannon and Nancy Tweedle, volunteers
at the Paso Robles Area Historical Society
were instrumental in providing information

from the archives. I could not have done this without their help. Additionally, when I presented my first edition of this book to them, they kindly asked me who I writing this book for. This caused me to completely refocus and rewrite the entire thing. For that I will be forever grateful. Additionally my friend, Mary Qualls introduced me to Colleen Craig who came up with the title of this book. That helped me shift my focus which lead me to rewrite the entire book. Wow. Rachel Poutasse, a volunteer at the Yolo County Historical Society researched land records and provided much needed information.

My cousin Sharon Freeman Kelly found letters from our dear relatives and they were so appreciated. In addition, her local knowledge and good memory added much context. Our meetings and conversations were delightful. Thanks, Sharon.

You know who else? My husband and foil, the Rayman. Without him, this book would not be a thing. He gave me the space, we took the trip, and what a great time it was! Plus, he didn't throw me from the train!

Linda Gibson provided editing help and I think she singlehandedly found over one thousand items that needed attention… many were spacing issues. Now I'm spaced out!

As a person interested in writing, I joined several writing groups and found help and information on the art of the deal. Anne R, Allen was a great help as were they all. Listening to what they wrote, gave me courage to continue. As did reading various non-fiction books that remain unlisted in the bibliography. Those authors gave me ideas as well.

In our trip across the country, we met many people in various historical societies that were cheerful, helpful, and interesting. Though I have few names to mention, the volunteers at these societies provided us and other visitors with loads of local knowledge that kept us interested and engaged. They were and are worth their weight in gold!

The members of the Oregon-California Trails Association that I interacted with were par excellence. octa-trails.org Bob Black has written guides that helped us find wagon wheel ruts. Various other members were unmet in person but very helpful with emails, videos, magazines and the like. The same may be said about Trails West, another fantastic organization that works to educate and inform. emigranttrailswest.org

U.S. National Park Service employees across the country were simply the best. A font of information was at their fingertips. The books and art presented were valuable and helpful too.

There were as many unnamed helpers as helpers. I only wish I had written more names down. And apologize if I failed to mention others that helped along the way.

About the Author

Born in Atascadero, California, Dianna (Thomas) Jackson grew up in Paso Robles, California. After writing blogs from 2010 to present, she decided her family history was worth telling. The history of the Dresser family includes angst, humor, grit, and determination And humor. She currently resides in Portland, Oregon with her husband, Ray aka Rayman and their Labradoodle, Beau. And as she is prone to say, "You can't make this stuff up."

This is her second book of non-fiction.

Made in the USA
Las Vegas, NV
07 September 2024

94915205R10203